The Hidden Face of Terrorism

The Dark Side of Social Engineering, From Antiquity to September 11

By

Paul David Collins

ISBN: 1-4033-6798-1 (E-book)
ISBN: 1-4033-6799-X (Paperback)

This book is printed on acid free paper.

1stBooks - rev. 09/23/02

In our modern world, discomforting truths are usually discarded in favor of fictions. One such fiction is the idea that terrorists are disenfranchised dissidents who independently generate the wealth and resources necessary for their heinous acts. Such is the contention of Professor Mark Juergensmeyer. In his article "Understanding the New Terrorism", Juergensmeyer says that modern terrorism "appears pointless since it does not lead directly to any strategic goal..." (158).

Juergensmeyer arrives at this conclusion because he restricts his examination to the visible perpetrators, whose motives may be, in fact, irrational. However, he does not examine the patrons of terrorism. Given the exceptional subtlety and discretion of terrorism's shadowy sponsors, Juergensmeyer may just be oblivious to their existence. On the other hand, Juergensmeyer could simply be parroting his fellow academicians in order to maintain the status quo. Whatever the case may be, this contention seems to be the overall view held by the orthodoxy of academia. With such a view vigorously promulgated by the arbiters of the dominant national paradigm, few can recognize those shady individuals who stand to profit from terrorist acts.

To understand terrorism, one must discard the view that arbitrarily characterizes it as "a resort to violence or a threat of violence on the part of a group seeking to accomplish a purpose against the opposition of constituted authority" (Adler, Mueller, and Laufer, 2001, pg. 309). Such an impotent notion is predicated upon the hopelessly flawed accidentalist perspective of history. It relegates terrorism, which is the product of conscious effort and design, to the realm of circumstantial spontaneity. In other words, a contrived act suddenly becomes an inexplicable social phenomenon.

In November 1989, Father Ignacio Martin-Baro, a social psychologist delivered a speech in California on "The Psychological Consequences of Political Terror" (Chomsky, 1992, pg. 386). In his speech, Martin-Baro gave a much more precise definition of terrorism, one that is ignored only at great peril. Noam Chomsky provides a synopsis of this speech:

He (Martin-Baro) stressed several relevant points. First, the most significant form of terrorism, by a large measure, is state terrorism-that is, "terrorizing the whole population through systematic actions carried out by the forces of the state." Second, such terrorism is an essential part of a "government-imposed sociopolitical project" designed for the needs of the privileged (pg. 386).

Disturbing though it may be, Martin-Baro's definition is one validated by history. The majority of terrorism throughout history has found its sponsors in the hallowed halls of officialdom, in the entity known as government. Terrorism is surrogate warfare, a manufactured crisis designed to induce social change. Its combatants consciously or unconsciously wage the war on behalf of higher powers with higher agendas. Whether its adherents are aware of it or not, terrorism always serves the ambitions of another.

In his article, "Fake Terror-The Road to Dictatorship," Michael Rivero states: "It's the oldest trick in the book, dating back to Roman times; creating the enemies you need" (pg. 1). The strategy is quite simple: Individuals create a crisis so that they can then introduce their desired solution. Several different theorists have delineated this plan throughout history. One such theorist was Freemason Albert Pike in his book *Morals and Dogma of the Ancient and Accepted Scottish Rite of Freemasonry Prepared for the Supreme Council of the Thirty-Third Degree for the Southern Jurisdiction of the United States and Published by Its Authority.*

Today, Freemasonry is considered little more than a harmless fraternity. However, researchers who have done serious study into the writings of prominent Freemasons and Freemasonic doctrine have found otherwise. In *Fire in the Minds of Men*, Librarian of Congress James H. Billington writes:

...Masonry was deliberately used by revolutionaries in the early nineteenth century as a model and a recruiting ground for their first conspiratorial experiments in political organization (pg. 93).

Author Jim Keith states:

Far from the innocuous ritual-based men's club that they are presented as in the mainstream media, Freemasonry has long been linked to international political manipulation, and has been alleged to be a conduit for the intentions of a number of elitist interests, including the House of Rothschild and their international banking connections (*Casebook on Alternative Three,* 1994, pg. 20).

One example of Freemasonic terrorism is the assassination of Archduke Ferdinand. Notes from the October 12, 1914 examination of the Archduke's assassin Cabrinovic reveal this connection:

President of the military court: "Tell me something more about the motives. Did you know, before deciding to attempt the assassination, that Tankosic and Cignovic were Freemasons? Had the fact that you and they were Freemasons an influence on your resolve?"

Cabrinovic: "Yes."

The President: "Did you receive from them the mission to carry out the assassination?"

Cabrinovic: "I received from no one the mission to carry out the assassination. Freemasonry had to do with it because it strengthened my intention. In Freemasonry it is permitted to kill. Cignovic told me that the Freemasons had condemned the Archduke Franz Ferdinand to death more than a year before" (Carr, 1958, pg. 77).

Canadian Naval Commander William Guy Carr states the following concerning these notes:

Tankosic and Cignovic were higher Masons than Cabrinovic. It had been previously brought out at the trial that Cignovic had told Cabrinovic that the Freemasons could not find men to carry out the Archduke's murder (pg. 77).

Count Czerin, an intimate friend of the Archduke, wrote in *Im-Welt-Krieg*:

"The Archduke knew quite well that the risk of an attempt on his life was imminent. A year before the war he informed me that the Freemasons had resolved on his death" (quoted in Carr, pg. 77).

In *Deterring Democracy*, Noam Chomsky gives an example of modern Freemasonic terrorism:

In July 1990, President Cossiga of Italy called for an investigation of charges aired over state television that the CIA had paid Licio Gelli to foment terrorist activities in Italy in the late 1960s and the 1970s. Gelli was grandmaster of the secret Propaganda Due (P2) Masonic lodge and had long been suspected of a leading role in terrorism and other criminal activities. In those years, according to a 1984 report of the Italian Parliament, P2 and other neo-fascist groups, working closely with elements of the Italian military and secret services, were preparing a virtual coup to impose an ultra-right regime and to block the rising forces of the left. One aspect of these plans was a "strategy of tension" involving major terrorist actions in Europe. The new charges were made by Richard Brenneke, who claims to have served as a CIA contract officer and alleged that the CIA-P2 connections extended over more than twenty years and involved a $10 million payoff (pg. 333).

Having established Freemasonry's involvement in terrorism, one returns to Freemasonic writer Albert Pike. In *Morals and Dogma*, Pike writes:

> The ROYAL SECRET, of which you are Prince, if you are a true Adept, if knowledge seems to you advisable, and Philosophy is, for you, radiant with a divine beauty, is that which the Sohar terms The Mystery of the BALANCE. It is the Secret of the UNIVERSAL EQUILIBRIUM...(pg. 859).

Occult expert and researcher Texe Marrs explains the Masonic concept of equilibrium:

> What is the high-level Masonic initiate chosen for world service told of the Royal Secret, the word

Equilibrium? He is instructed that the Illuminati is continually creating and fostering two opposing forces which clash and compete. Chaos is produced by the friction between these two, polar ideologies or groups. And it is through chaos that The Plan for global domination and the self-realization of deity is executed. The heated battle that ensues results, finally, in Equilibrium—the syncretic balance of the two opposing forces. In all occult systems since the beginning of time, this system of achieving Equilibrium through the planned conflict of opposites is found (Marrs, 1995, pg. 94-96).

The Royal Secret of Freemasonry, encapsulated in the word Equilibrium, represents the ultimate product of crisis exploitation. The crisis may be either genuine or, as is most often the case, contrived. Either way, the emergency always proves advantageous for those desiring the revolutionary transformation of human civilization. In short, the Masonic notion of equilibrium is radical societal modification through expedient crisis control. Pike states that, through this Royal Secret, the world will be transformed into a Masonic-dominated kingdom. He writes:

> Such, my Brother, is the TRUE WORD of a Master
> Mason; such the true ROYAL SECRET, which makes
> possible, and shall at length make real, the HOLY
> EMPIRE of true Masonic Brotherhood (pg. 861).

Jan Kozak, a member of the Secretariat of the Communist Party of Czechoslovakia, outlined the same strategy sans the Freemasonic mysticism. In his book *And Not a Shot is Fired, the Communist Strategy for Subverting a Representative Government*, Kozak describes "revolutionary parliamentarianism" or "the pincer movement." Kozak explains:

> A preliminary condition for carrying out
> fundamental social changes and for making it possible
> that parliament be made use of for the purpose of

transforming a capitalistic society into a socialistic one, is:

a. to fight for a firm parliamentary majority which would ensure and develop a strong 'pressure from above,' and

b. to see to it that this firm parliamentary majority should rely on the revolutionary activity of the broad working masses exerting 'pressure from below' (Kozak, 1957, pg. 16).

Researcher Ralph Epperson elaborates:

The first step consisted of having the conspiracy's own people infiltrate the government (the "pressure from above.")

The second step was to create a real or alleged grievance, usually through either an action of government or through some situation where the government should have acted and didn't.

The third step consisted in having a mob created by the real or alleged grievance that the government or the conspiracy caused demand that the problem be solved by a governmental action (the "pressure from below.")

The fourth step consisted in having the conspirators in the government remedy the real or alleged situation with some oppressive legislation.

The fifth step is a repeat of the last three. The government does not solve the problem and the mob demand more and more legislation until the government becomes totalitarian in nature by possessing all of the power (Epperson, 1985, pg. 37).

History is replete with examples of manufactured terrorism for revolutionary objectives. Marcus Licineus Crassus, a wealthy politician in Rome, lived long before the likes of Pike and Kozak.

However, it seems that he understood how to capitalize on a crisis. Michael Rivero reveals:

> Just to give you an idea of what sort of man Crassus really was, he is credited with invention of the fire brigade. But in Crassus' version, his fire-fighting slaves would race to the scene of a burning building whereupon Crassus would offer to buy it on the spot for a tiny fraction of it's worth. If the owner sold, Crassus' slaves would put out the fire. If the owner refused to sell, Crassus allowed the building to burn to the ground. By means of this device, Crassus eventually came to be the largest single private landholder in Rome, and used some of his wealth to help back Julius Caesar against Cicero (Rivero, 2001, pg. 1).

However, Crassus' crowning achievement was his conquest of Rome. Once again, Crassus exploited a grievance. This time, however, the exigency was one he had created. In 70 B.C., Rome had a Republican form of government. The rule of law had been established and there were "very strict limits on what Rulers could do, and more importantly NOT do" (Rivero, 2001, pg. 1). Crassus, Rivero asserts: "had no intentions of enduring such limits to his personal power, and contrived a plan" (pg.1).

This plan exploited the slave revolt led by Spartacus. Spartacus "had no intention of marching on Rome itself, a move he knew to be suicidal" (Rivero, 2001, pg. 1). Spartacus and his group planned to escape Rome by hiring a mercenary fleet to sail them well beyond the empire's grasp (pg.1). Crassus had different designs in mind for Spartacus and his band of slaves, designs that would deliver Rome into the wealthy politician's hands. Crassus:

> ...bribed the mercenary fleet to sail without Sparticus (sic), then positioned two Roman legions in such a way that Sparticus had no choice but to march on Rome (Rivero, 2001, pg. 1).

The population of Rome reacted by handing over the power of the government to Crassus. No longer was he simply a politician of minor significance. Crassus was now Rome's Praetor. The year following Spartacus' defeat, Crassus became Consul of Rome (Rivero, 2001, pg. 1). Rivero writes:

> With this maneuver, the Romans surrendered their Republican form of government. Soon would follow the first Triumvirate, consisting of Crassus, Pompeii, and Julius Caesar, followed by the reign of the god-like Emperors of Rome.
>
> The Romans were hoaxed into surrendering their Republic, and accepting the rule of Emperors (pg.2).

Many years later, an ambitious German Chancellor named Hitler would make his bid for power through terror. His strategy was remarkably similar to the tactics employed by Crassus. Hitler's brown shirt lackeys:

...staged beatings, set fires, caused as much trouble as they could, while Hitler made speeches promising that he could end the crime wave of subversives and terrorism if he was granted extraordinary powers.

The Germans were hoaxed into surrendering their Republic, and accepting the rule of Der Fuhrer (Rivero, 2001, pg. 3).

The crowning achievement of Hitler's *coup detat* on freedom was the burning of the Reichstag. The official line touted by court historians is that the Reichstag fire was started by "a half-witted Dutch Communist with a passion for arson" named Marinus van der Lubbe (Shirer, 1959, pg. 192). However, William Shirer reveals in his monumental book *The Rise and Fall of the Third Reich*:

...it was established at the subsequent trial at Leipzig that the Dutch half-wit did not possess the means to set so vast a building on fire so quickly. Two and a half minutes after he entered, the great central hall was fiercely burning. He had only his shirt for tinder. The main fires, according to the testimony of experts at the trial, had been set with considerable quantities of chemicals and gasoline. It was obvious that one man could not have carried them into the building, nor would it have been possible for him to start so many fires in so many scattered places in so short a time (pg. 193).

The real masterminds were revealed during the Nuremberg trial. Shirer speaks of the revelation:

> The idea for the fire almost certainly originated with Goebbels and Goering. Hans Gisevius, an official in the Prussian Ministry of the Interior at the time, testified at Nuremberg that "it was Goebbels who first thought of setting the Reichstag on fire," and Rudolf Diels, the Gestapo chief, added in an affidavit that

"Goering knew exactly how the fire was to be started" and ordered him "to prepare, prior to the fire, a list of people who were to be arrested immediately after it." General Franz Halder, Chief of the German General Staff during the early part of World War II, recalled at Nuremberg how on one occasion Goering had boasted of his deed (pg. 193).

Halder testified:

At a luncheon on the birthday of the Fuehrer in 1942 the conversation turned to the topic of the Reichstag building and its artistic value. I heard with my own ears when Goering interrupted the conversation and shouted: "The only one who really knows about the Reichstag is I, because I set it on fire!" With that he slapped his thigh with the flat of his hand (Shirer, 1959, pg. 193).

If the half-wit Dutch communist was not the mastermind behind this terrorist act, what exactly was his place in the overall plan? Again, Shirer provides the sobering answer to that question:

> Van der Lubbe, it seems clear, was a dupe of the Nazis. He was encouraged to try to set the Reichstag on fire. But the main job was to be done-without his knowledge, of course-by the storm troopers (pg. 193).

These revelations came much too late for the German people. Hitler "lost no time in exploiting the Reichstag fire to the limit (Shirer, 1959, pg. 194)". It was time for the Nazis to commence what researcher Ralph Epperson referred to as step four in the process of steering society down a totalitarian path. Author Shirer describes the assault on anti-authoritarian big mouths:

> On the day following the fire, February 28, he (Hitler) prevailed on President Hindenburg to sign a decree "for the Protection of the People and the State"

suspending the seven sections of the constitution which guaranteed individual and civil liberties (pg. 194).

This venomous decree presented the following:

Restrictions on personal liberty, on the right of free expression of opinion, including freedom of the press; on the rights of assembly and association; and violations of the privacy of postal, telegraphic and telephonic communications; and warrants for house searchers, orders for confiscations as well as restrictions on property, are also permissible beyond the limits otherwise prescribed (pg. 194).

Furthermore, Shirer states:

In addition, the decree authorized the Reich government to take over complete power in the federal states when necessary and imposed the death sentence for a number of crimes, including "serious disturbances of the peace" by armed persons (pg. 194).

Chancellor Hitler also used the Nazis' acts of terror to shift power from the representative government of Germany to the Nazis. This shift came on March 23, 1933 with the passing of the Enabling Act. Shirer writes an accurate description of this act:

Its five brief paragraphs took the power of legislation, including control of the Reich budget, approval of treaties with foreign states and the initiating of constitutional amendments, away from Parliament and handed it over to the Reich cabinet for a period of four years. Moreover, the act stipulated that the laws enacted by the cabinet were to be drafted by the Chancellor and "might deviate from the constitution" (pg. 198).

While Hitler tried to promote his regime as some form of democratic egalitarianism, it is obvious from the evidence that he was transmogrifying Germany into a fascist dictatorship. Although the above examples are very compelling, they are rather dated as well. Are there more recent and modern examples of state-sponsored terrorism? Moreover, are there any examples of state-sponsored terrorism in America? Unfortunately, the answer to that question seems to be yes.

The first example is in the year 1962. The chairman of the Joint Chiefs of Staff, Lyman L. Lemnitzer, and his fellow JCS members wanted to remove Castro from Cuba. Exactly what interests Lemnitzer and his fellow warhawks represented are unclear. However, one thing is apparent: these military men considered Castro an impediment to be expunged by means of overt war. According to former Washington Investigative Producer for ABC, James Bamford, the Joint Chiefs of Staff planned to engineer several terrorist acts to instigate war:

According to secret and long-hidden documents obtained for Body of Secrets, the Joint Chiefs of Staff drew up and approved plans for what may be the most corrupt plan ever created by the U.S. government. In the name of anticommunism, they proposed launching a secret and bloody war of terrorism against their own country in order to trick the American public into supporting an ill-conceived war they intended to launch against Cuba.

Codenamed Operation Northwoods, the plan, which had the written approval of the Chairman and every member of the Joint Chiefs of Staff, called for innocent people to be shot on American streets; for boats carrying refugees fleeing Cuba to be sunk on the high seas; for a wave of violent terrorism to be launched in Washington, D.C., Miami and elsewhere. People would be framed for bombings they did not commit; planes would be hijacked. Using phony evidence, all of it would be blamed on Castro, thus giving Lemnitzer and his cabal the excuse, as well as the public and international backing, they needed to launch their war (pg. 82).

By no means do these revelations exonerate Castro. He stands condemned by the historical record as a tyrannical despot. Since 1959, this communist dictator has ruled Cuba with an iron fist. Certainly, fictions did not have to be concocted to denounce Castro. However, Lemnitzer was not willing to let Castro's deeds and actions speak for him. In fact, Lemnitzer and his collaborators believed that America's existing rivalry with Cuba had to be further exasperated to graphically illustrate the threat of Castro. Bamford elaborates:

"World opinion, and the United Nations forum," said a secret JCS document, "should be favorably affected by developing the international image of the Cuban government as rash and irresponsible, and as an alarming and unpredictable threat to the peace of the Western Hemisphere" (Bamford, 2001, pg. 83).

Under Operation Northwoods, not even the space program would have been safe:

One idea seriously considered involved the launch of John Glenn, the first American to orbit the earth. On February 20, 1962, Glenn was to lift off from Cape Canaveral, Florida, on his historic journey. The flight was to carry the banner of America's virtues of truth, freedom, and democracy into orbit high over the planet. But Lemnitzer and the Chiefs had a different idea. They proposed to Lansdale that, should the rocket explode and kill Glenn, "the objective is to provide irrevocable proof that…the fault lies with the Communists et al Cuba [sic]." This would be accomplished, Lemnitzer continued, "by manufacturing various pieces of evidence which would prove electronic interference on the part of the Cubans." Thus, as NASA prepared to send the first

American into space, the Joint Chiefs of Staff were preparing to use John Glenn's possible death as a pretext to launch a war (Bamford, 2001, pg. 84).

Operation Northwoods even called for the military turning in on itself:

> Among the actions recommended was "a series of well coordinated incidents to take place in and around" the U.S. Navy base at Guantanamo Bay, Cuba. This included dressing "friendly" Cubans in Cuban military uniforms and then have them "start riots near the main gate of the base. Others would pretend to be saboteurs inside the base. Ammunition would be blown up, fires started, aircraft sabotaged, mortars fired at the base with damage to installations" (Bamford, 2001, pg. 84).

Operation Northwoods would draw upon history as well, using the 1898 explosion aboard the battleship *Maine* in Havana harbor as inspiration:

> "We could blow up a U.S. ship in Guantanamo Bay and blame Cuba," they proposed; "casualty lists in U.S. newspapers would cause a helpful wave of national indignation" (Bamford, 2001, pg. 84).

The proposal targeted Florida and Washington as well:

> "We could develop a Communist Cuban terror campaign in the Miami area, in other Florida cities and even Washington," they wrote. "The terror campaign could be pointed at Cuban refugees seeking haven in the United States...We could sink a boatload of Cubans en route to Florida (real or simulated)...We could foster attempts on lives of Cuban refugees in the United States even to the extent of wounding in

instances to be widely publicized" (Bamford, 2001, pg. 84-85).

President Kennedy obviously saw Operation Northwoods for the illegal act of treason it was and denied the proposal. It was not too long there after that the bloodthirsty chairman lost his job (Bamford, 2001, pg. 88-89). Lemnitzer "may have thought that all copies of the relevant documents had been destroyed..." (pg. 88). However, they were not and landed in the National Archive where James Bamford would find them years later. The story can now be told of how the United States government planned to perpetrate acts of terror on its own people.

The attempt to create a Cuban terrorist threat makes it clear that our government has no reservations about using state-sponsored terrorism to achieve its ends. However, it is in the Oklahoma City bombing of 1995 that one sees the tangible enactment of modern day state-sponsored terrorism. Many Americans have been taught that loners Timothy McVeigh and Terry Nichols, fueled by militia-inspired conspiracy theories and white supremacist propaganda, perpetrated one of the worst terrorist acts in American history all by themselves. Journalist Ambrose Evans-Pritchard directs our attention to a little known fact that places this notion in doubt. That fact is that McVeigh had made a telephone call to the white separatist commune known as Elohim City two weeks before the bombing (Evans-Pritchard, 1997, pg. 36). Researcher Jim Keith also reveals a connection between McVeigh and Elohim City:

...the accused bomber (Timothy McVeigh) was aware of Elohim City and, according to sources in the government quoted by the New York Times and Reuters, had visited the compound about two weeks before the bombing on April 5. McVeigh was also stopped for a traffic violation about 20 miles from Elohim City and, according to federal officials, telephone records show that the accused bomber called the compound on April 16, as well as four minutes after reserving the Ryder truck allegedly employed in the bombing (*OKBomb!*, 1996, pg. 123).

"Pastor" Robert Millar runs Elohim City. In *The Secret Life of Bill Clinton*, Evans-Pritchard allows a glimpse at the philosophy motivating Millar and his racist disciples:

> His (Millar) eccentric religion is known as Christian Identity, a British import from the 1870s. Drawing heavily on the "ancestral memory" theories of Carl Jung, the movement asserts that the white peoples of Europe are the lost tribes of Israel. Jews are deemed to be "half-devil" descendants of the "serpent seed," a union of Eve and Satan. The Jewish diaspora is the instrument of Satan to achieve dominion over the world-notably, by means of the United Nations.
>
> Blacks do not fare well either in the eschatology of the cult. They are the cohorts of Satan. Before the end of the world in A.D. 2000, there will be a final

confrontation between the Aryans and Satan's Jews. Asians are "mud" people.

It is race theology of the most fevered kind, laced with millenarian prophesy from the Old Testament and Wiccan nature worship (pg. 40).

The mainstream, corporate-controlled media has attempted to blame the bombing on fundamentalist Christians ever since April 19, 1995. Any honest and detailed examination of the Scriptures invariably reveals a belief system that is antithetical to Millar's perverse "religion." The idea of mixing Christianity with Wicca is considered an anathema by Christians and Wiccans alike. Moreover, many individuals and groups oppose the United Nations for legitimate reasons. Historically, the global organization has undermined the sovereignty of nation-states and orchestrated bloodbaths under the guise of "peacekeeping missions." However, imbecilic racists seeking to validate their own hateful beliefs developed the notion of the United Nations as a "Jewish world conspiracy". In short, Millar's Weltanschauung exhibits several disproportionate anomalies that may have been introduced by external parties for the purpose of manipulation. Who the hidden manipulators are will be examined later.

The story of Elohim City's involvement in the Oklahoma City bombing begins with ATF informant Carol Howe. In 1994, Howe "jumped off a wall to escape a group of black youths and broke both her heels" (Evans-Pritchard, 1997, pg. 54). Fueled with racial hatred by her experience, Howe called a hotline set up by one Dennis Mahon (pg. 54). Mahon is a former Imperial Dragon of the Ku Klux Klan. Eventually Mahon left the Klan and "graduated to the Aryan Nations, the descendant of the fascist Silver Shirts" (pg. 46). In 1996, Mahon would give a five-hour long confession to involvement in the Oklahoma City bombing in January 1996 (pg. 50). This confession was given to J.D. Cash, a freelance reporter. Evans-Pritchard examines this interview:

At the time, Cash was in touch with The Jubilee, the far-right publication of the Christian Identity movement. He had been invited to speak about the Oklahoma bombing at a Jubilee conference, and his picture had appeared in the monthly newspaper next to that of Louis Beam, the *eminence grise* of the Aryan movement. When Mahon saw the picture, he falsely assumed that Cash was an emissary sent Louis Beam.

"I went along with it. If he was going to be that dumb, that was fine by me," explained Cash. "So I said to him:'Dennis, why did you blow up the fucking building in broad daylight with a nursery in there? You've no idea how much trouble you've caused the movement, killing all those children.'

"'I know, the whole thing's fucked up.'

"'Dead babies don't cause revolutions. There are some people who are real upset about this.'"

Over the next five hours Mahon worked his way through a bottle of Irish whisky and babbled frantically about the bombing. In the flood of conflicted emotions, he lurched from guilt, to pride, to a perverse jealousy.

The former Imperial Dragon could not bear to see an upstart Nazi like Timothy McVeigh hogging the limelight, taking all the *credit* for the bombing.

"The thing you have got to understand about Mahon is that he had become a joke in the movement," said Cash. "He was being ridiculed as a talker, and he wanted to prove that he was a 'doer.' It was his middle-aged crisis, I guess" (pg. 50).

Evans-Pritchard continues:

Before leaving, Cash pulled out his tape-recorder and asked Mahon if he wanted to convey any messages to Tim McVeigh in prison. (Cash had a letter from McVeigh's lawyers scheduling an interview with the prisoner.) Mahon fell for the bait. Speaking into the microphone, he exhorted McVeigh to accept his "sacrifice," even if he was guilty by reason of entrapment. Don't forget Waco; don't forget Ruby

Ridge; don't forget all the southerners who died for the cause; and don't forget that members of his family were vulnerable to reprisal.

Immediately afterward, J.D. Cash gave a sworn deposition to Stephen Jones, the lawyer of Timothy McVeigh, recording the ramblings of the Imperial Dragon. It was submitted to the court in Denver, where it has remained sealed ever since (pg. 51).

In an interview with Evans-Pritchard, Mahon made remarks suggesting he was in the employ of the government:

"I don't know, Dennis. A lot of people are beginning to think you work for the Bureau."

"They are? I wouldn't work for those clowns. They need me in this town, all right. If I go, they'll lose half their staff. I threatened to leave the state and they said, 'No, no, don't go, it'll put us out of business.' So I asked them for a commission."

"I can believe that, Dennis."

"Now the CIA, that's a different matter; that's a good organization," he said, holding his thoughts for a moment while he ordered the biggest plate of food on the menu. We were at Tally's, a Lebanese café in Tulsa where he tended to his Iraqi contacts. "You paying for this?"

"Anything you want."

"Just checking, although I'm flush right now. You should see how much money the CIA's putting into my Swiss bank account."

"Yes, Dennis."

"$3,000 a month"(pg. 43-44).

Later, Mahon would brag to the journalist about receiving protection from the government: "'Yes, I know I'm protected,' Mahon told me archly. 'It's a nice feeling to have'" (pg. 51).

Things went sour between Mahon and Howe when Mahon allegedly raped Carol (Evans-Pritchard, 1997, pg. 54). Carol fled to her grandfather's ranch in Texas in hopes of escaping Mahon only to receive several threatening calls on her answering machine (pg. 54). The problems with Mahon eventually compelled Carol to first file a complaint with Tulsa Police's hate crimes unit and then file for an emergency protective order with the Tulsa County District Court (pg. 54). The Tulsa County District Court contacted the Tulsa office of the ATF (pg. 54). According to Evans-Pritchard: "They pounced immediately" (pg.54).

Carol went to work for the ATF gathering information on Mahon and White Aryan Resistance (Evans-Pritchard, 1997, pg. 55). Mahon and White Aryan Resistance (or WAR) had been training and stockpiling weapons for a race war and war with the government (pg. 55). This training and stockpiling was going on at Elohim City (pg. 55). Mahon would eventually take Carol to Elohim City (pg. 56). At this point, the ATF became less interested in Mahon and more on Elohim City:

By now the focus was already shifting from Mahon to Elohim City. Carol's early reports had been so disturbing that the ATF wanted her to infiltrate the cult, find out what kind of weaponry they had, and profile key radicals (Evans-Pritchard, 1997, pg. 56).

On orders from the ATF, Carol befriended and eventually became the girlfriend of Andreas Strassmeir (Evans-Pritchard, 1997, pg. 59). Strassmeir was:

...a former German infantry officer who had gained entry into the U.S. neo-Nazi movement and established himself as the chief of security at Elohim City, the movement's paramilitary headquarters in eastern Oklahoma (Evans-Pritchard, 1997, pg. 35).

Strassmeir was suspected by many to be working for the government. Andreas "attended the meetings of the Texas Light

Infantry militia, until he was chased off as a suspected undercover agent" (Evans-Pritchard, 1997, pg. 81). Another source pointing to Strassmeir's links to the government was Mike Vanderboegh, a member of the *1ˢᵗ Alabama Calvary Regiment*, a militia. The story is told in *The Secret Life of Bill Clinton:*

He (Vanderboegh) was drawn into the Oklahoma bombing case in late 1995 when he sat down for a coffee with a federal agent in Birmingham, Alabama. It was a cordial meeting. Vanderboegh's militia group had done a favor for the Feds, helping them crack a case involving theft from a military base.

"He pulled out a piece of paper with the name, social security number, and profile of Andreas Strassmeir," recalled Vanderboegh. "He said, 'We've gone as far as we can with this; we've been told to back off. Maybe you guys can do something with it.' Then he told me Strassmeir had been the government-sponsored snitch inside the Oklahoma bombing. He walked me through the whole thing" (pg. 35).

Even Strassmeir's colleague in the crusade for white supremacy, Dennis Mahon, suspected the German had connections in government. He certainly hated at it in his interview with Ambrose Evans-Pritchard:

"It looks like Andreas has put you in a bit of a spot, Dennis."

"You think he's an agent?"

"Makes sense."

"Yeah, that little shit's going to get himself killed. You know Andy told me he'd been in the GSG-9."

"Strassmeir told you that? He told you he'd worked for German counter-terrorism?"

"Yeah, told me he worked on the Baader-Meinhoff gang in the eighties. This was a guy who could infiltrate, I tell you, he knew his stuff, but I thought he was just going after the Communists," said Mahon, chewing on the inside of his cheek. "Funny thing. He was never curious about the people in my album. His car kept breaking down, and he couldn't travel. Never even had a telephone."

"Good cover."

"You think so?"

"That's exactly what you'd do if you were a deep penetration agent, isn't it, Dennis?"

"Yeah, maybe. I hope to God he wasn't working as an agent over here" (pg. 45).

Carol began to collect a steady stream of intelligence indicating that Strassmeir and Mahon were planning to blow up a building. By Christmas, Mahon and Strassmeir:

...had picked three possible targets for attack in the state of Oklahoma: the IRS and federal buildings in Tulsa, and the "federal building" in Oklahoma City. Carol has stated under oath that she reported these threats to her ATF case officer. "I wrote down about blowing up federal buildings," she testified. "I relayed it the way we relayed it" (Evans-Pritchard, 1997, pg. 60).

As time went on, the fact that an attack on the Alfred P. Murrah building in Oklahoma was coming became more apparent:

She (Howe) later said she informed the ATF, on paper, that something called the "Morrow Building" (sic) had been mentioned as one of the targets (Evans-Pritchard, 1997, pg. 60).

Among the evidence of foreknowledge was:

...an FBI write-up of her (Howe) debriefing on April 21, 1995, at the FBI's OKBOMB command center in Oklahoma City. It said that Dennis Mahon had discussed "targeting federal installations for destruction through bombings, such as the IRS Building, the Tulsa Federal Building."

She said that Strassmeir and Mahon had "taken three trips to Oklahoma City in November 1994, December 1994, and February 1995." She had accompanied the group once, in December 1994 (Evans-Pritchard, 1997, pg.60).

By February 1995, the ATF was ready to conduct a raid on Elohim City to arrest Andreas Strassmeir (Evans-Pritchard, 1997, pg. 62-63). The ATF:

...had requested INS "participation in [the] raid," because Strassmeir was an illegal alien. The Oklahoma Highway Patrol had been alerted that Andreas Strassmeir "carries a .45 auto pistol at all times...if he is stopped and has the gun on him, ATF will file the charges" (Evans-Pritchard, 1997, pg. 63).

Then the unbelievable happened:

> But the FBI muscled in and prevented the arrest. On February 22, 1995, Agent Finley (Howe's case officer) was notified by the Oklahoma Highway Patrol that the "FBI also had an ongoing investigation at Elohim City." One can imagine the shock of this rookie ATF agent when she discovered that she had unwittingly stumbled on a much bigger sting being conducted by the FBI, probably a counterintelligence operation approved at the highest levels in Washington. For whatever reason, Strassmeir was being protected by the Bureau (Evans-Pritchard, 1997, pg. 63).

In an interview with Evans-Pritchard, Strassmeir produced disturbing revelations concerning his involvement with the government:

I told Strassmeir outright that the evidence linking him to the bombing was very strong.

"Either you are a mass murderer, or you are an undercover agent," I said. "Either you killed all those people, or you risked your life to penetrate a group of vile, dangerous people. Take your pick, Andreas, but don't think you can stick your head in the sand and hope that it will all go away. It won't go away."

"You don't understand," he said.

"You know what I think already," I persisted. "I think you're a very courageous man. I think you did everything you could to stop that bombing. You did your part; you got inside the most deadly terrorist conspiracy in the history of the United States; you got these maniacs to believe in you; your cover was brilliant; and somebody let you down, didn't they Andreas?"

"You don't understand," he repeated almost plaintively.

"I do understand, Andreas. I understand that it wasn't your fault. Are you listening to me? It wasn't your fault. So why not just come out and tell the whole rotten truth, and get it over and done with? You don't have to cover for the ATF."

"You think it's as simple as that?" he stammered.

"I don't know, Andreas. You tell me. Who were you working for anyway? Did the Germans send you over?"

"No! No, they would never do that."

"So who was it then? The ATF? The Bureau? Who were you working for?"

"Look, I can't talk any longer."

"Just listen to me, Andreas. They're going to hang you out to dry. When this thing comes down they're going to leave you holding that bomb, or—and you know this as well as I do—you'll fall under a train one day on the U Bahn, when nobody's looking."

"I've got to go to work."

"There comes a time in every botched operation when the informant has to speak out to save his own skin, and that's now, Andreas."

"How can he?" he shouted into the telephone. "What happens if it was a sting operation from the very beginning? What happens if it comes out that the plant was a provocateur?"

"A provocateur?"

"What if he talked and manipulated the others into it? What then? The country couldn't handle it. The relatives of the victims are going to go crazy. He's going to be held responsible for the murder of 168 people."

"That is true."

"Of course the informant can't come forward. He's scared shitless right now."

"It sounds to me as if you've got a problem, Andreas."

"*Scheise*" (Evans-Pritchard, 1997, pg. 91-92).

Even the head of Elohim City, Pastor Millar, was on the government's payroll. The first indication of this came from a discussion between Carol Howe and Millar of WAR's planned uprising. Evans-Pritchard reports:

> Interestingly, this was not seen as an ethnic uprising. Pastor Millar was in contact with Louis Farrakhan's organization, as well as militant Hispanic and American Indian groups. He explained to Carol that "Elohim City would unite with other races in order to create a more powerful adversary opposing the U.S. government. The white supremacist issues are secondary to the anti-government attitude" (pg. 57-58).

Millar's willingness to subordinate the white supremacist aims to achieve more of an anarchistic goal does not fit the traditional mold of a racist. It does, however, fit that of someone trying to incite civil unrest that the government could then exploit. All doubt was eventually removed: "He had been recruited as an FBI informant several years earlier. That stunning revelation would come out later in a Tulsa courtroom" (Evans-Pritchard, 1997, pg. 43).

This is not the first case of the government protecting a dangerous, racist organization. Jim Keith gives yet another example:

If the idea of the FBI actually fostering violent right wing groups is alien, reflect on the following. In July 1993, there were reports of an FBI agent using the name Reverend Joe Allen through whose activities as an agent provocateur 100 persons had been convicted since 1977, and Allen opened a gymnasium in Los Angeles which he decorated with Nazi paraphernalia and, according to the *L.A. Times*, provided skinheads free admittance to the gym as well as funding for White supremacist activities. In the meantime, Allen was videotaping skinheads making pipe bombs at his gym, and their buying of illegal weaponry. Allen reportedly encouraged the skinheads to plot assassinations against Blacks and Jews, but was in fact setting the conspirators up for an FBI raid in which eight arrests were made. The skinheads were arrested on charges of weapons violations and the plot to kill L.A. ethnic leaders (*OKBOMB!*, 1996, pg. 125).

What came out of the Oklahoma City bombing? Jan Kozak's "pressure from above" went to work and passed oppressive legislature in the form of the *Antiterrorism and Effective Death Penalty Act of 1996*. This act made no one safer and threw the Fourth Amendment to the Constitution in the wastebasket. The pincers clamped down a little bit harder on the American people.

Presently, America finds itself in the midst of a tumultuous conflict because of the September 11, 2001 terrorist attacks on the Pentagon and the World Trade Center. This begs the obvious question: was this attack state-sponsored? Remember the earlier contention that the majority of terrorism is state-sponsored. Terrorists just do not have the resources, the money, or the expertise without the aid of a government or factions within a government. It is still too early to know all of the facts and details surrounding the events of September 11. However, there is evidence suggesting that the attack was no exception to the rule. The investigation of government complicity begins with an examination of the evidence for government foreknowledge. Warnings were received at the highest levels of government. A May 16, 2002 Associated Press release reported:

> President Bush was told by U.S. intelligence in advance of the Sept. 11 attacks that Osama bin Laden's terrorist network might hijack American airplanes, the White House acknowledged Wednesday night (pg. 1).

The article continues:

> The development, first reported by CBS News, comes as congressional investigators intensify their

study of whether the government failed to respond adequately to warnings of suicide hijackings before Sept. 11. It is the first direct link between Bush and intelligence gathered before Sept. 11 about the attacks (pg. 1)

The press release also states that one senior administration official:

...speaking on condition of anonymity, said the president was made aware of the potential for hijackings of U.S. planes during one or more routine intelligence briefings last summer (pg. 1)

The media spin-doctors have tried to turn this damning revelation around in the Bush Administration's favor. Many court reporters of the Establishment press have attempted to argue that the information was simply too fragmentary to know for sure that such a major attack was planned. However, the evidence favors the contrary. An abundance of reliable warnings was received. When compiled, these warnings provided a clear enough picture that the government could have acted upon to prevent the September 11 tragedy. A few significant examples will suffice in proving this point.

David Schippers can hardly lay claim to the derisive stigma of "wide-eyed conspiracy theorist." He is a respected lawyer credited with toppling several prominent organized crime figures in New York. He led the impeachment campaign against former President William Jefferson Clinton and has several ties to Washington political power players. Schippers appeared on the October 10, 2001 *Alex Jones Show* to address some recurring questions about the September 11 attacks. In the following exchange between Jones and Schippers, the dialogue shifts to the topic of prior knowledge:

Alex Jones: Now later you got it [Warning of the attacks-ADDED] from FBI agents in Chicago and Minnesota that there was going to be an attack on lower Manhattan.

David Schippers: Yea—and that's what started me calling. I started calling out there. First of all, I tried to see if I could get a Congressman to go to bat for me and at least bring these people out there and listen to them. I sent them information and nobody cared. It was always, "We'll get back to you", "we'll get back to you", "we'll get back to you". Then I reached out and tried to get to the Attorney General, when finally we got an attorney general in there that I would be willing to talk to. And, again, I used people who were personal friends of John Ashcroft to try to get him. One of them called me back and said, "Alright I have talked to him. He will call you tomorrow morning." This was like a month before the bombing. The next morning I got a call. It wasn't from Ashcroft. It was from somebody in the Justice Dept.

Alex Jones: One of his handlers.

David Schippers: Yea, and I started telling him the situation and he said, "You know we don't start our investigations at the top." I said I would like to talk to the Attorney General because this is vital. He said, "We don't start our investigations at the top. Let me look into this and I will get back to you." As I sit here today, I have never heard from him (2001, pg. 1-2).

Warnings may have even come from the mouth of the enemy. In July of 2001, Bin Laden was hospitalized in an American hospital in Dubai for a kidney infection (Rose, 2001, pg. 1). According to the French newspaper *Le Figaro*, much more happened than just kidney treatment:

...a CIA agent met Osama bin Laden in a Gulf hospital as recently as last July and received "precise information" about an imminent attack on the U.S.

According to the French daily, the agent met Bin Laden while he was being treated at the American Hospital in Dubai for a kidney infection. The agent was subsequently recalled to Washington.

The hospital today vigorously denied the report, which is based on a number of sources, including French secret services and a hospital administrator (Rose, 2001, pg.1).

However, the story goes even deeper:

In a further twist, French secret service operatives are said to have met officials from the US embassy in Paris last August after the arrest of Algerian Djamel Beghal in the UAE.

A French secret service report on 7 September warned of possible attacks and that the order to act would come from Afghanistan. Le Figaro says very precise information on targets for attack was communicated to the CIA (Rose, 2001, pg. 1-2).

A *Financial Times* article by Gwen Robinson seems to indicate that French secret service warnings were not the only ones the CIA ignored. In the article, Robinson reports:

> A former US intelligence agent has alleged that the CIA ignored detailed warnings he passed on in 1998 that a Gulf state was harbouring an al—Qaeda cell led by two known terrorists (pg. 1).

These allegations, according to Robinson, come from one Robert Baer, "a former case officer in the CIA's directorate of operations" (pg. 1). Baer has written a book entitled *See No Evil*, which explores these allegations. Robinson gives a brief overview:

> Among fresh details are an account of how, after he left the CIA in 1997 and became a consultant in

Beirut, Mr. Baer was advising a prince in a Gulf royal family.

A military associate of the prince, he said, had last year warned Mr Baer that a "spectacular terrorist operation" was being planned and would take place shortly.

Mr Baer said he also provided him a computer record of "hundreds" of secret al—Qaeda operatives in the Gulf region, many in Saudi Arabia (pg. 1).

All of this information was passed on from Robert to the CIA. However, Robinson states flatly: "The information Mr Baer gave to the CIA was not followed up, he (Baer) said" (pg. 2). Why would the Central Intelligence Agency do nothing with critical information concerning one of the world's most infamous terrorist organizations?

These and several other eye-opening revelations have many asking why the U.S. government did not move to stop Bin Laden and the al-Qaeda. This question can be answered with a question: why move against Bin Laden and the al-Qaeda if they are your assets? The story of the dreaded al-Qaeda terrorist network actually begins with Zbigniew Brzezinski, President Carter's national security advisor. In his 1997 book, *The Grand Chessboard: American Primacy and Geostrategic Objectives*, Brzezinski provides readers with the motivation for the creation of a terrorist threat. He begins:

> The last decade of the twentieth century has witnessed a tectonic shift in world affairs. For the first time ever, a non-Eurasian power has emerged not only as a key arbiter of Eurasian power relations but also as the world's paramount. The defeat and collapse of the Soviet Union was the final step in the rapid ascendance of a Western Hemisphere power, the United States, as the sole and, indeed, the first truly global power…(1997, pg. xii).

Brzezinski celebrates the fact that America is being transformed into a world empire. However, he identifies a distinct threat to

America's ascendancy to the position of sole global power: "The attitude of the American public toward the external projection of American power has been much more ambivalent" (Brzezinski, 1997, pg. 24). Apparently, the citizenry's aversion towards imperialistic policies, which Brzezinski euphemistically interprets as ambivalence, is an obstacle to the empire's expansion. After all, there are still plenty of patriots who understand that Brzezinski's expansionistic "geostrategy" is irreconcilable with the tenets of Americanism.

This sense of awareness has been a major obstacle to the foreign policy elites that Brzezinski represents. Thus far, enough patriots know that none of the Freedom Documents (i.e., the Constitution, Bill of Rights, etc.) make concessions for the arbitrary extension of America's authority through brutish military expeditions. As a sovereign nation itself, America is supposed to honor the autonomy of other countries and is not to initiate militaristic campaigns unless she is threatened. Yet, Brzezinski believes that adherence to such principles could provoke world wide social upheaval:

America's withdrawal from the world or because
the sudden emergence of a successful rival—would
produce massive international instability. It would
promote global anarchy (1997, p.30).

Brzezinski continues on in his own hyperbolic fashion:

Without sustained and directed American
involvement, before long the forces of global disorder
could come to dominate the world scene (1997, p.194).

In other words, the promotion and practice of representative
government amongst other nations would lead to doomsday itself. In
such statements, the former national security advisor reveals the
authoritarian features of his bizarre eschatology. According to
Brzezinski's Weltanschauung, those who cherish individual liberties
and the sovereignty of their respective nations constitute the "forces
of global disorder." Therefore, these forces must be defeated or they
will invariably cause the apocalypse. However, Brzezinski fails to

mention that such a doomsday would only mean the end for him and his elitist comrades. Therefore, public opinion must be altered. At this pivotal juncture, Brzezinski cites a very interesting historical example:

> The public supported America's engagement in
> World War II largely because of the shock effect of the
> Japanese attack on Pearl Harbor (1997, p. 25).

Ah, an option presents itself! Mass consensus could be facilitated through mass trauma. In fact, the engineering of widespread compliance is an essential constituent in the implementation of Brzezinski's foreign policy. In an exemplary moment of self-incrimination so endemic to elitist tracts, Brzezinski pens a damning confession:

> Moreover, as America becomes an increasingly
> multi-cultural society, it may find it more difficult to
> fashion a consensus on foreign policy issues, except in

the circumstance of a truly massive and widely perceived direct external threat (1997, pg. 211).

A readily exploitable menace, whether genuine or promulgated, is the solution. Brzezinski began the construction of his "direct external threat" years before *The Grand Chessboard* was written. In an interview with the French magazine *Le Nouvel Observateur,* the former national security advisor made a stunning confession that will change the history books forever:

Q: The former director of the CIA, Robert Gates, stated in his memoirs ["From the Shadows"], that American intelligence services began to aid the Mujahadeen in Afghanistan 6 months before the Soviet intervention. In this period you were the national security adviser to President Carter. You therefore played a role in this affair. Is that correct?

Brzezinski: Yes. According to the official version of history, CIA aid to the Mujahadeen began during 1980, that is to say, after the Soviet army invaded Afghanistan, 24 Dec 1979. But the reality, secretly guarded until now, is completely otherwise: Indeed, it was July 3, 1979 that President Carter signed the first directive for secret aid to the opponents of the pro-Soviet regime in Kabul. And that very day, I wrote a note to the president in which I explained to him that in my opinion this aid was going to induce a Soviet military intervention.

Q: Despite this risk, you were an advocate of this covert action. But perhaps you yourself desired this Soviet entry into war and looked to provoke it?

B: It isn't quite that. We didn't push the Russians to intervene, but we knowingly increased the probability that they would (Blum, 1998, pg. 1)

Having encouraged the Soviets to invade Afghanistan, Brzezinski now had a pretext for radicalizing and arming a population that would be used at a future date as a "direct external threat" to the United States. Part of the radicalization process included the brainwashing of children under the guise of education. *The Washington Post's* Joe Stephens and David B. Ottaway report:

> In the twilight of the Cold War, the United States spent millions of dollars to supply Afghan schoolchildren with textbooks filled with violent images and militant Islamic teachings, part of covert attempts to spur resistance to the Soviet occupation.
>
> THE PRIMERS, which were filled with talk of jihad and featured drawings of guns, bullets, soldiers and mines, have served since then as the Afghan school system's core curriculum. Even the Taliban used the American-produced books, though the radical

movement scratched out human faces in keeping with

its strict fundamentalist code (2002, pg. 1-2).

Stephens and Ottaway identify the governmental and educational

organizations involved in the development of the textbooks:

> Published in the dominant Afghan languages of
> Dari and Pashtu, the textbooks were developed in the
> early 1980s under an AID [Agency for International
> Development-ADDED] grant to the University of
> Nebraska-Omaha and its Center for Afghanistan
> Studies. The agency spent $51 million on the
> university's education programs in Afghanistan from
> 1984 to 1994 (2002, pg. 4).

Under this project, the images and talk of violence were craftily

intermingled with legitimate education:

Children were taught to count with illustrations showing tanks, missiles and land mines, agency officials said. They acknowledged that at the time it also suited U.S. interests to stoke hatred of foreign invaders (2002, pg. 4).

One aid worker's examination of a textbook produced shocking results: "An aid worker in the region reviewed an unrevised 100-page book and counted 43 pages containing violent images or passages (2002, pg. 5)". The writers of *The Washington Post* story go on to provide a specific example of the material that is nothing less than appalling:

One page from the texts of that period shows a resistance fighter with a bandolier and a Kalashnikov slung from his shoulder. The soldier's head is missing.

Above the soldier is a verse from the Koran. Below is a Pashtu tribute to the mujaheddin [sic], who are described as obedient to Allah. Such men will sacrifice their wealth and life itself to impose Islamic law on the government, the text says (2002, pg. 5-6).

This social engineering project successfully transformed Muslim children into conscienceless killing machines. Many would go on to join al-Qaeda, the terrorist network headed up by Osama bin Laden. An heir to Saudi construction fortune, Bin Laden went to Afghanistan in 1979 to fight the Soviets (Moran, 2001, pg. 2). Bin Laden eventually came to head the Maktab al-Khidamar, also known as the MAK (pg. 2). It was through this front organization that money, arms, and fighters were supplied to the Afghan war (pg. 2).

However, according to MSNBC's Michael Moran, there is more to the story:

What the CIA bio conveniently fails to specify (in its unclassified form, at least) is that the MAK was nurtured by Pakistan's state security services, the Inter-Services Intelligence agency, or ISI, the CIA's primary conduit for conducting the covert war against Moscow's occupation (pg. 2).

Even after the war Bin Laden was on good terms with the CIA:

> Though he has come to represent all that went wrong with the CIA's reckless strategy there, by the end of the Afghan war in 1989, bin Laden was still viewed by the agency as something of a dilettante-a rich Saudi boy gone to war and welcomed home by the Saudi monarchy he so hated as something of a hero (Moran, 2001, pg. 3).

Bin Laden would later receive three necessary provisions from factions of government. These essentials would allow him and al-Qaeda to conduct one of the worst terrorist attacks ever conceived. These constituents were: 1.) Protection courtesy of highly influential, well-placed shepherds in government, 2.) Government funding, and

3.) Government training. Without a beat, individuals in positions of authority delivered.

Both democrat and republican administrations protected Bin Laden. Undaunted by Osama's attack on the USS Cole and bombing of the embassies, this nonpartisan aegis consistently insulated the terrorist and his network. President William Jefferson Clinton, a democrat, shielded Bin Laden and company from the hand of justice in Sudan. Mansoor Ijaz revealed this fact in the December 5, 2001 *Los Angeles Times*:

President Clinton and his national security team ignored several opportunities to capture Osama bin Laden and his terrorist associates, including one as late as last year.

I know because I negotiated more than one of the opportunities.

From 1996 to 1998, I opened unofficial channels between Sudan and the Clinton administration. I met with officials in both countries, including Clinton, U.S. National Security Advisor Samuel R. "Sandy" Berger and Sudan's president and intelligence chief. President Omar Hassan Ahmed Bashir, who wanted terrorism sanctions against Sudan lifted, offered the arrest and extradition of Bin Laden and detailed intelligence data about the global networks constructed by Egypt's Islamic Jihad, Iran's Hezbollah and the Palestinian Hamas.

Among those in the networks were the two hijackers who piloted commercial airliners into the World Trade Center.

The silence of the Clinton administration in responding to these offers was deafening (pg. 1).

Sudan offered Bill Clinton the ideal opportunity to apprehend Bin Laden and prevent future terrorist attacks. Instead, the U.S. pressured Sudan to make Bin Laden leave "despite their [the Sudanese-ADDED] feeling that he could be monitored better in Sudan than elsewhere" (Ijaz, 2001, pg. 1-2). It was off to Afghanistan for Bin Laden and his merry, marauding band of cutthroats and murderers:

> Bin Laden left for Afghanistan, taking with him Ayman Zawahiri, considered by the U.S. to be the chief planner of the Sept. 11 attacks; Mamdouh Mahmud Salim, who traveled frequently to Germany to obtain electronic equipment for Al Qaeda; Wadih El-Hage, Bin Laden's personal secretary and roving emissary, now serving a life sentence in the U.S. for his role in the 1998 U.S. embassy bombings in Tanzania and Kenya; and Fazul Abdullah Mohammed and Saif Adel, also accused of carrying out the embassy attacks.
>
> Some of these men are now among the FBI's 22 most—wanted terrorists (Ijaz, 2001, pg. 2).

In Afghanistan, the Taliban protected Bin Laden and his Al Qaeda network. There is an odd symmetry revealed through this relationship.

Both Bin Laden and the Taliban were little more than a creation of the CIA. Selig Harrison, a South Asian expert from the Woodrow Wilson International Center for Scholars, made this known at a conference in London. *The Times of India* records Harrison's revelations:

> LONDON: The Central Intelligence Agency (CIA) worked in tandem with Pakistan to create the "monster" that is today Afghanistan's ruling Taliban, a leading US expert on South Asia said here.
>
> "I warned them that we were creating a monster," Selig Harrison from the Woodrow Wilson International Centre (sic) for Scholars said at the conference here last week on "Terrorism and Regional Security: Managing the Challenges in Asia."
>
> Harrison said: "The CIA made a historic mistake in encouraging Islamic groups from all over the world to come to Afghanistan." The US provided $3 billion for building up these Islamic groups, and it accepted

Pakistan's demand that they decided how this money should be spent, Harrison said.

Harrison, who spoke before the Taliban assault on the Buddha statues was launched, told the gathering of security experts that he had meetings with CIA leaders at the time when Islamic forces were being strengthened in Afghanistan. "They told me these people were fanatical, and the more fierce they were the more fiercely they would fight the Soviets," he said.

"I warned them that we were creating a monster" (pg. 1).

To the average American, the Taliban might have been a rogue gallery of maniacs that comprised a fanatical outlaw government and nothing more. However, Harrison makes it clear that the Taliban was a well-coordinated intelligence project:

"The Taliban are not just recruits from 'madrassas' (Muslim theological schools) but are on the payroll of the ISI (Inter—Services Intelligence, the intelligence wing of the Pakistani government)" (*The Times of India*, pg. 2).

According to Mansoor Ijaz, yet another opportunity to capture Bin Laden arose even after the terrorist had left Sudan. This time an Arab nation was willing to turn over Bin Laden:

In July 2000, three months before the deadly attack on the destroyer Cole in Yemen...I brought the White House another plausible offer to deal with Bin Laden, by then known to be involved in the embassy bombings. A senior counter—terrorism official from one of the United States' closest Arab allies...an ally whose name I am not free to divulge...approached me with the proposal after telling me he was fed up with the antics and arrogance of U.S. counter—terrorism officials.

The offer, which would have brought Bin Laden to the Arab country as the first step of an extradition process that would eventually deliver him to the U.S., required only that Clinton make a state visit there to personally request Bin Laden's extradition. But Senior Clinton officials sabotaged the offer, letting it get caught up in internal politics within the ruling family…Clintonian diplomacy at its best (pg. 2).

Clinton departed from the White House and made way for a republican administration under the new President, George W. Bush. As the famous song by *The Who* goes: "Meet the new boss, same as the old boss." FBI efforts to investigate the Bin Laden families' connection to terrorism were thwarted by the Bush administration. In an article for the *London Guardian*, journalist Greg Palast presents clear evidence of government obfuscation. Palast writes:

FBI documents shown on BBC Newsnight last and obtained by The Guardian show that they had earlier sought to investigate two of Osama bin Laden's relatives in Washington and a Muslim organisation (sic), the World Assembly of Muslim Youth (WAMY), with which they were linked.

The FBI file, marked Secret and coded 199, which means a case involving national security, records that Abdullah bin Laden, who lived in Washington, had originally had a file opened on him "because of his relationship with the World Assembly of Muslim Youth—a suspected terrorist organisation (sic) ("FBI and US Spy Agents Say Bush Spiked Bin Laden Probes Before September 11", pg. 1).

In an interview on BBC's Newsnight, national security expert Joe Trento elaborated on the terrorist connections to WAMY:

They've had connections to Osama Bin Laden's people. They've had connections to Muslim cultural and financial aid groups that have terrorist connections. They fit the pattern of groups that the Saudi royal family and Saudi community of princes— the 20,000 princes—have funded who've engaged in terrorist activity.

Now, do I know that WAMY has done anything that's illegal? No, I don't know that. Do I know that as far back as 1996 the FBI was very concerned about this organisation (sic)? I do (Palast, "Has Someone been sitting on the FBI?" pg. 3).

The preponderance of evidence should have led to a full-scale investigation. However, Palast informs us that it did not:

But the FBI files were closed in 1996 apparently before any conclusions could be reached on either the Bin Laden brothers or the organisation (sic) itself.

High—placed intelligence sources in Washington told the Guardian this week: "There were always constraints on investigating the Saudis."

They said the restrictions became worse after the Bush Administration took over this year. The intelligence agencies had been told to "back off" from investigations involving other members of the Bin Laden family, the Saudi royals, and possible Saudi links to the acquisition of nuclear weapons by Pakistan.

"There were particular investigations that were effectively killed."

Only after the September 11 attacks was the stance of political and commercial closeness reversed towards the other members of the large Bin Laden clan, who have classed bin Laden as their "black sheep" ("FBI and US Spy Agents Say Bush Spiked Bin Laden Probes Before 11 September" pg. 1).

Certainly, operating under the protective wings of deliberate mismanagement and presidential complicity proved most advantageous to Bin Laden and his network. However, as the old adage goes, "Money makes the world go round." Without the facilitative constituent of financing, Osama's plans would have been complicated many times over. The trail of complicit government funding begins with former ISI director-general Lt.-Gen. Mahmud Ahmad. In *The Times of India*, Manoj Joshi reports:

NEW DELHI: While the Pakistani Inter Services Public Relations claimed that former ISI director-general Lt-Gen Mahmud Ahmad sought retirement after being superseded on Monday, the truth is more shocking.

Top sources confirmed here on Tuesday, that the general lost his job because of the "evidence" India produced to show his links to one of the suicide bombers that wrecked the World Trade Centre. The US authorities sought his removal after confirming the fact that $100,000 were wired to WTC hijacker Mohammed Atta from Pakistan by Ahmad Umar Sheikh at the instance of Gen Mahumd (sic)(pg. 1).

Ahmad's contribution to the hijackers not only shows involvement on the part of factions in the Pakistani government. It also casts suspicion upon the CIA. Under treaty, the head of Pakistani ISI must be approved by the American Director of Central Intelligence, suggesting that Pakistan's intelligence organization is supervised by a mere CIA puppet. Selig Harrison, the South Asia expert for the Woodrow Wilson International Center for Scholars, holds that the marriage between the American CIA and the Pakistani ISI is alive and well today:

The old associations between the intelligence agencies continue, Harrison said. "The CIA still has close links with the ISI (Pakistan's Inter—Services Intelligence)" (*The Times of India*, pg. 2).

The final component in transforming the Bin Laden network into an effective "direct external threat" is training. Some of the terrorists did, in fact, receive training courtesy of the government. This now-confirmed revelation came out in *The Washington Post* and *Newsweek* (Wheeler, 2001, pg. 1). Larry Wheeler repeats the reports in the *Pensacola News Journal:*

As many as four of 19 suspected hijackers may have participated during the 1990s in the (Pensacola) base's flight training program for foreign military trainees, according to reports in The Washington Post and Newsweek magazine (pg. 1).

Wheeler takes a closer look at the reports:

The Newsweek article says U.S. military officials gave the FBI information suggesting that five of the alleged hijackers received training in the 1990s at secure U.S. military installations.

It says three of them listed their address on driver licenses and car registrations as 10 Radford Blvd. on Pensacola NAS, a base road on which residences for foreign—military flight trainees are located.

Those suspects are:

Saeed Alghamdi, believed to have helped hijack United Airlines Flight 93 that crashed in rural Pennsylvania.

Ahmad Alnami, who also was aboard Flight 93.

Ahmed Alghamdi, who is suspected of helping commandeer United Airlines Flight 75, which hit the south tower of the World Trade Center.

Saeed Alghamdi listed the address in March 1997 to register a 1998 Oldsmobile; five months later, he used the same address to register a late—model Buick.

The other two used the address on the driver licenses issued in 1996 and 1998.

The Newsweek article cited two other suspects with possible U.S. military training: One may have been trained in strategy and tactics at the Air War College in Montgomery, Ala., and one may have received language training at Lackland Air Force Base in San Antonio.

A Washington Post article adds a fourth suspect who may have trained in Pensacola:

Hamza Alghamdi, who also is believed to have been aboard Flight 75 (pg. 2-3).

Wheeler also informs us that such training of foreigners is nothing new:

It's not unusual for foreign nationals to train at Pensacola—area bases.

Pensacola NAS and Whiting Field train many of the more than 6,000 foreign military students who receive flight training each year at U.S. military institutions.

The students are instructed in everything from warfare specialty training to air navigation meteorology and land/water survival…(pg. 2).

It is very strange that the Navy would train individuals with such questionable backgrounds. Those who authorized the tutelage of these suspicious characters would almost certainly be well aware of their dubious personal histories. Certainly, the trainees' radical views would not have escaped the scrutiny of the very government that was now training them. In the very least, their beliefs would have excluded them from instruction in skills that could easily be exploited to achieve criminal ends. Cognizance of these facts and their explosive ramifications suggests that shadowy interests in positions of authority stood to gain from the training of potential terrorists.

Those hijackers who were not trained at military bases received their training at flight schools. This went on with the blessings of federal authorities, as is evidenced by the fact that the FBI knew that the terrorists were using the flight schools. Reporters Steve Fainaru and James V. Grimaldi disclosed the following in *The Washington Post*:

> Federal authorities have been aware for years that suspected terrorists with ties to Osama bin Laden were receiving flight training at schools in the United States and abroad, according to interviews and court testimony (2001, pg. 1)

The reporters also stated that this fact came from a government source:

> A senior government official yesterday acknowledged law enforcement officials were aware that fewer than a dozen people with links to bin Laden had attended U.S. flight schools (2001, pg. 1).

Fainaru and Grimaldi go on to list various instances in which the FBI knew of terrorists training at flight schools here in the United States:

In 1996, two flight school operators said last week, FBI agents visited them to obtain information about several Arab pilots connected to a Pakistani terrorist eventually convicted of plotting to bomb U.S. airliners.

The flight schools, Coastal Aviation of New Bern, N.C., and Richmor Aviation of Schenectady, N.Y., were two of four that provided flight training to Abdul Hakim Murad in the early 1990s, according to Philippine authorities. Murad was arrested in Manila in 1995 and later convicted in New York of plotting to blow up a dozen U.S. airliners over the Pacific, then crash a suicide plane into CIA headquarters.

In 1998, FBI agents questioned officials from Airman Flight School in Norman, Okla., about a graduate later identified in court testimony as a pilot for bin Laden, according to Dale Davis, the school's director of operations.

This year, the trial of bin Laden associates for the 1998 bombings of U.S. embassies in Kenya and Tanzania yielded documents containing several references to flight schools and bin Laden pilots.

Two weeks before the Sept. 11 attack, Davis said, FBI agents returned to Norman seeking information about another Airman student, a French-Moroccan dropout who had entered the country on a visa sponsored by the flight school. The man, Zacarias Moussaoui, had been detained in Eagan, Minn., on an immigration violation after he tried to purchase time on a jet simulator…even though he had never flown solo in a single-engine aircraft (2001, pg. 1).

In light of this shocking information, the obvious question becomes: If the federal authorities knew that terrorists were training at flight schools, why was no action taken to stop them? Evidently, powerful individuals wanted insurance that the terrorists could murder innocent people and destroy national landmarks with a high degree of proficiency.

The preponderance of evidence rules out the possibility of gross negligence on the part of the government. The government had all the means necessary to detect and prevent the attacks. Researcher Russ Kick makes a significant statement concerning this point:

> The US has the Central Intelligence Agency, the Federal Bureau of Investigation, the National Security Agency, the Defense Intelligence Agency, the National Reconnaissance Office, the Secret Service, and a host of other intelligence and security agencies. These agencies employ Echelon, which monitors the majority of electronic communication in the world; Carnivore, which intercepts email; Tempest, a technology that can read a computer monitor's display from over a block away; Keyhole satellites that have a resolution of four

inches; and other spy technologies, probably most of which we don't know about. In 2001, the US spent $30 billion on intelligence gathering and an additional $12 billion on counterterrorism. With all these resources, and more, we're supposed to believe that the government didn't have the slightest inkling that terrorists were planning to attack the United States, much less hijack planes and send them careening into major landmarks (2002, pg. 1).

After reviewing the facts, one must consider a more sinister possibility: Certain factions in the United States government created the Bin Laden menace and actually desired the attacks. Whether Moran realizes it or not, his article "Bin Laden Comes Home to Roost" reveals evidence that the Agency may have been equipping Bin Laden's network for purposes other than fighting the Soviets:

The CIA, ever mindful of the need to justify its "mission," had conclusive evidence by the mid-1980s of the deepening crisis of infrastructure within the Soviet Union. The CIA, as its deputy director Robert Gates acknowledged under congressional questioning in 1992, had decided to keep that evidence from President Reagan and his top advisors and instead continued to grossly exaggerate Soviet military and technological capabilities in its annual "Soviet Military Power" report right up to 1990 (pg. 4).

Now, a troubling question arises. Given the impending collapse of the Soviet Union and the inexorable demise of communism, Bin Laden's involvement in the crusade against the Soviets seems inconsequential. More succinctly, it is irrelevant. Yet, despite his axiomatic obsolescence in the anti-communist campaign, Bin Laden continued to receive funds. Since such financing did not represent an investment in the ongoing war with the Soviets, there must have been ulterior motives for maintaining Bin Laden's network.

What was the true agenda that motivated the CIA to support what would later become an international Frankenstein monster? Former CIA Associate Deputy Director of Operations Theodore Shackley may have already answered this question in his book, *The Third Option: An Expert's Provocative Report on an American View of Counterinsurgency Operations*:

> Senior intelligence officers like myself, who had experience in paramilitary operations, have always insisted that the United States should also consider the third option: the use of guerrilla warfare, counter-insurgency techniques and covert action to achieve policy goals...Political warfare is very often the stitch in time that eliminates bloodier and more costly alternatives (pg. 17).

It is possible that the September 11 attack represents a tangible enactment of Shackley's third option. Bin Laden's ties to the intelligence community certainly reinforce such a contention. Was the al—Qaeda and Bin Laden considered part of a third option to facilitate political and social change in the United States?

Consider a conversation that took place between former DEA agent Michael Levine and a CIA agent. It suggests that the CIA is ready and willing to use the third option in America. This discourse is recorded in *The Triangle of Death*:

> "How can you be so good at what you do and have so little understanding of what really pulls your strings? Don't you realize that there are factions in your government that want this to happen—an emergency situation too hot for a constitutional government to handle."
>
> "To what end?" I asked.
>
> "A suspension of the Constitution, of course. The legislation is already in place. All perfectly legal. Check it out yourself. It's called FEMA. Federal Emergency Management Agency. 'Turn in your guns,

you antigovernment rabble rousers. And who would be king, Michael?"

"CIA," I said (pg. 353).

In an interview with William Norman Grigg, Levine made it clear that this account was not fictitious:

> According to Levine, this shocking exchange is not the product of an imagination fed by alarmists. "That scenario…came from a specific conversation I had with a CIA officer in Argentina in 1979," Levine informed The New American. "There was a small group of us gathered for a drinking at the CIA guy's apartment. There were several Argentine police officers there as well; at the time, Argentina was a police state in which people could be taken into custody without warning, tortured, and then 'disappeared.'"

"At one point my associate in the CIA said that he preferred Argentina's approach to social order, and that America should be more like that country," Levine continues. "Somebody asked, 'Well, how does a change of that sort happen?' The spook replied that it was necessary to create a situation of public fear—a sense of impending anarchy and social upheaval..."(pg. 11).

Terrorism in the United States is one of the methods that have been employed to generate the changes desired by Levine's CIA friend. It has provided a pretext for the introduction of draconian laws and measures previously unthinkable. Representative Henry Gonzalez recognized this fact when he made the following comment:

The truth of the matter is that you do have those standby provisions, and the statutory emergency plans are there whereby you could, in the name of stopping terrorism, apprehend, invoke the military, and arrest

Americans and hold them in detention camps (Cuddy, 1999, pg. 164).

Add to the list of "statutory emergency plans" the USA Patriot Act, passed in response to the September 11 attacks. According to *Washington Post* Staff Writer Jim McGee, this law:

...empowers the government to shift the primary mission of the FBI from solving crimes to gathering domestic intelligence. In addition, the Treasury Department has been charged with building a financial intelligence-gathering system whose data can be accessed by CIA.

Most significantly, the CIA will have the authority for the first time to influence FBI surveillance operations inside the United States and to obtain evidence gathered by federal grand juries and criminal wiretaps (2001, pg. 1-2).

McGee also informs us that this act:

>...effectively tears down legal fire walls erected 25 years ago during the Watergate era, when the nation was stunned by disclosures about presidential abuses of domestic intelligence-gathering against political activists (2001, pg. 2).

The legal bulwarks to which McGee refers were erected as a result of the Church hearings. These pivotal hearings were chaired by Senator Frank Church. McGee revisits the Church Hearings:

>After wading through voluminous evidence of intelligence abuses, a committee led by Sen. Frank Church warned that domestic intelligence-gathering was a "new form of governmental power" that was unconstrained by law, often abused by presidents and always inclined to grow (2001, pg. 2).

The Church hearings led to several reforms. The Patriot Act nullifies many of those reforms. McGee explores this step backwards:

One reform that grew out of the Church hearings was the segregation within the FBI of the bureau's criminal investigation function and its intelligence-gathering against foreign spies and international terrorists.

The new anti-terrorism legislation foreshadows an end to that separation by making key changes to the law underpinning it, the Foreign Intelligence Surveillance Act (FISA) of 1978.

"They have had to divide the world into the intelligence side and law enforcement," (Assistant Attorney General) Chertoff said. The new law "should be a big step forward in changing the culture" (McGee, 2001, pg. 2-3).

What new culture would emerge as a result of the Patriot Act's implementation? McGee elaborates on Chertoff's new culture:

> FISA allows the FBI to carry out wiretaps and searches that would otherwise be unconstitutional. Unlike regular FBI criminal wiretaps, known as Title IIIs, the goal is to gather intelligence, not evidence. To guard against abuse, the attorney general had to certify to a court that the "primary purpose" of the FISA wiretap was to listen in on a specific foreign spy or terrorist.
>
> In negotiating the new legislation, the Bush administration asked for a lower standard for approval—changing the words "primary purpose" to "a purpose." This would allow people merely suspected of working with terrorists or spies to be wiretapped.
>
> The debate over this wording was one of the fiercest surrounding the new anti-terrorism law. Senate

negotiators settled on the phrase "a significant purpose," which will still allow the Bush administration the leeway it wants, according to Chertoff and others (McGee, 2001, pg. 3).

In other words, Chertoff's new culture is a police state. The Patriot Act is designed to transform America into a surveillance society. Wiretapping has been expanded to invade the privacy of a larger portion of the populace. In the name of fighting terrorism, the prying eyes of the government can now watch those merely deemed "suspicious." Furthermore, wiretaps are no longer just a tool in criminal investigations. Under the US Patriot Act, they become a means of gathering information on the citizenry. Unfortunately, the surprises do not stop there. The act also lifts many of the constraints on the CIA's power. McGee writes:

The new law also gives the CIA unprecedented access to the most powerful investigative weapon in the federal law enforcement's arsenal: the federal grand jury. The grand juries have nearly unlimited power to gather evidence in secret, including testimony, wiretap transcripts, phone records, business records or medical records.

In the past, Rule 6(e) of the Rules of Federal Procedure required a court order whenever prosecutors shared federal grand jury evidence with other federal agencies.

The new law permits allows the FBI to give grand jury information to the CIA without a court order, as long as the information concerns foreign intelligence or international terrorism. The information can also be shared widely throughout the national security establishment.

"As long as the targets are non-Americans, they now can sweep up and distribute, without limitation, the information they gather about Americans," said Morton Halperin, a leading member of the civil liberties community and co-author of a legal text on national security law (McGee, 2001, pg. 4).

The *Washington Post* writer also points to the CIA moving slowly but surely into the domestic realm:

> As a legal matter, the CIA is still prohibited from exercising domestic police powers or spying on U.S. citizens. However, its intelligence officers will work side by side with federal agents who do have arrest and domestic investigative authority (2001, pg. 5).

Whether or not any of these measures will prove affective in the war on terror has yet to be seen. Will they actually result in the end of the dreaded al-Qaida network? Although the new anti-terrorist campaign is still young, an examination of its forerunners leaves one with little hope. Ironically, the precursory system to this newly implemented one only fostered al-Qaida and its allied terrorist network. One thing is abundantly clear: the Patriot Act is setting the

Paul David Collins

stage for the building of a huge intelligence apparatus that can be used to watch and police the people. The Founding Fathers fervently warned against such concentration of power.

On December 18, 2000, Bush made the following remark on CNN's *Newsday*: "If this were a dictatorship, it'd be a heck of a lot easier, just so long as I'm the dictator" (pg. 1). In the wake of the US Patriot Act and other "anti-terrorism initiatives", blueblood Bush just might receive his wish. It seems that Big Brother is being built all in the name of national security. Of course, the Bush Administration has tried to paint critics of their plans as fear—mongering paranoids. Even more sinister, opponents of the Bush regime's moves have found themselves labeled disciples of Bin Laden and potential terrorists. Attorney General John Ashcroft's statements before the Senate Judiciary Committee were most telling:

> To those…who scare peace—loving people with phantoms of lost liberty, my message is this: Your tactics only aid terrorists, for they erode our national

unity and diminish our resolve. They give ammunition to America's enemies and pause to America's friends. They encourage people of good will to remain silent in the face of evil (Page, 2001, pg. 10).

Chicago Tribune columnist Clarence Page interpreted Ashcroft's statements accurately: "In other words, get out of my way. You're either with us or you're with the terrorists" (2001, pg. 10). The current administration has profited greatly from this tactic. According to a briefing in the July 7, 2002 *Springfield News-Sun*, legendary ex-cop and whistle-blower Frank Serpico received catcalls during a Fourth of July reading of the Declaration of Independence in Chatham (pg. 2). What had the heroic crime-fighter said to receive such a negative response? The briefing shares Serpico's words:

"It is my opinion that never before have we, as a nation, stood in greater danger of losing our individual liberties as we are today," he said. "We, the people of this great nation, are being punished for the transgressions of our leaders and their consorts" (2002,

pg. 2).

Frank Serpico is not a member of al-Qaeda or the Taliban. He is a former police officer who waged a war against departmental corruption that almost cost his life. Nevertheless, Ashcroft's elastic definition of "terrorist" has placed Serpico and other concerned Americans into the same category as Osama bin Laden. Of course, catcalls are the mildest form of censorship. A harder crackdown, one involving the strong arm of the government, could be one more terrorist attack away.

The acts of terrorism not only meant Big Brother for Americans, but bombs for Afghans. With the September 11 bombings, Bin Laden provided the pretext for an invasion of Afghanistan and an attempt to oust the Taliban. According to the BBC's George Arney, plans to oust the Taliban were already on the table before the September 11 attacks:

A former Pakistani diplomat has told the BBC that the US was planning military action against Osama Bin Laden and the Taleban even before last week's attacks.

Niaz Naik, a former Pakistani Foreign Secretary, was told by senior American officials in mid-July that military action against Afghanistan would go ahead by the middle of October.

Mr. Naik said US officials told him of the plan at a UN-sponsored international contact group on Afghanistan which took place in Berlin.

Mr. Naik told the BBC that at the meeting the US representatives told him that unless Bin Laden was handed over swiftly America would take military action to kill or capture both Bin Laden and the Taleban leader, Mullah Omar.

The wider objective, according to Mr. Naik, would be to topple the Taleban regime and install a transitional government of moderate Afghans in its place-possibly under the former Afghan King Zahir Shah (pg. 1-2).

The American officials Niaz Naik encountered obviously did not speak lightly. When action was taken against Afghanistan, the hammer came down hard. No target was spared in the attempt to capture or kill Bin Laden, civilians included. In an article in the *Toronto Sun*, Eric Margolis described some of the results of the "war on terrorism":

To date, the U.S. has dropped 10,000 bombs on Afghanistan, killing sizable numbers-in the range of 1,500-2,000, according to Afghan sources. U.S. bombing of cities, towns, and villages has driven over 160,000 people into refugee camps (pg. 1).

One would hope that the tremendous loss of life would somehow lead to a desirable outcome, namely the installation of a government that no longer fostered terrorists and recognized the rights of the

Afghans. If the means produced such an end, perhaps it could be argued that the massive sacrifices are somehow justifiable. However, this was not the case. While innocent Afghans were being killed, many of the culprits were escaping, courtesy of the United States and Pakistan. This was reported in *The Times*, a British newspaper:

> THE United States secretly approved rescue flights by Pakistan into Kunduz that let Taleban leaders and al-Qaeda fighters escape from the besieged northern Afghan city before its fall last year, *New Yorker* magazine reports today.
>
> US intelligence officials and military officers said that the Bush Administration approved the flights and ordered US Central Command to set up a special air corridor to ensure their safety to allow evacuation of Pakistani soldiers and intelligence men stranded by Northern Alliance victories (Bone, pg.1).

Paul David Collins

The *New Yorker* stated that Taleban and al-Qaeda members escaping was an "unintended consequence" of the evacuation (Bone, pg. 1). It is possible that the escape of these terrorists, while being a display of gross incompetence on the part of the United States, was unintended. However, given prior examples of America funding and protecting both the Taliban and al-Qaida, it seems highly unlikely. Could it be that "assets" were being protected so they could perpetrate more acts of terrorism that the political, military, and intelligence establishments could then exploit? It would certainly give ammunition to those who wish to carry on building Big Brother here at home while continuing with reckless interventionist policies abroad.

Escaping Taleban and al-Qaeda members were not the only problem with the "anti-terrorist" crusade in Afghanistan. The new government the United States installed in place of the Taleban was made up of anything but "moderate Afghans." The majority of this replacement government is made up of members of the Northern Alliance. According to Eric Margolis: "Of 30 cabinet seats, two-thirds went to Northern Alliance Tajiks, notably the power ministries of defence, the interior and foreign affairs" (pg. 1). Eric Margolis holds that cooperating with the Northern Alliance was "a colossal, inexcusable blunder" (pg. 1). He explains:

> On Dec. 3, 2000—one year ago—this column said that overthrowing the Taliban would "pave the way for a second Russian occupation of Afghanistan." This has now happened. The Northern Alliance, armed and funded by Russia, directed by the Afghan Communist party and under overall command of the chief of the Russian general staff, Marshall Viktor Kvashin, deputy KGB director Viktor Komogorov, and a cadre of Russian advisers, seized Kabul and all of northern Afghanistan (pg. 1).

Therefore, a closer examination reveals that the Northern Alliance is not an improvement over the Taleban. If anything, it represents a declivity. America's Faustian pact with the Northern Alliance has resulted in communism's covert reprisal of Afghanistan, all in the name of fighting terrorism. Margolis even points to the former Afghan king's involvement in this endeavor:

> The 87-year old deposed Afghan king, Zahir Shah, widely blamed for allowing the communists to infiltrate Afghanistan in the 1970s, was invited back as a figurehead monarch. In short, a communist-dominated regime, ruled by a king, whose strings are pulled by Moscow. Quite a bizarre creation (pg. 1).

Evidently, the replacement of the Taliban with a more democratic form of government was never the goal. After all, the communist puppets of the Northern Alliance are anything but torchbearers for liberty and freedom. Therefore, another motive must have necessitated the military expedition into Afghanistan. Returning to *The Grand Chessboard*, Brzezinski refers to an area known as the "Eurasian Balkans," a region that must be controlled in order to insure American primacy. Afghanistan is nestled comfortably within the

"Eurasian Balkans," thus making her a nation of geostrategic significance (1997, pg. 124). The United States military has made the world safe for the imperialist aspirations of western elites represented by Brzezinski.

Shortly after the horrible September 11 attacks, America was hit yet again with a wave of terrorism, this time taking the form of mysterious "anthrax letters." In her book, *Secret Agents: The Menace of Emerging Infections*, science and medical journalist Madeline Drexler describes the effects of anthrax:

> Anthrax begins mildly enough, with fever, fatigue, and sometimes a cough. What often follows are a few cruelly deceptive days of respite. All the while, toxins released in the bloodstream by bacteria are destroying cells and causing fluid to accumulate in tissues. Leaky blood vessels cause blood pressure to plummet and organs to fail. Then comes the fatal blow; abruptly

labored breathing followed, within a day or two, by shock leading to death (2002, pg. 234).

Who unleashed such a horrible form of bioterrorism? Once again, as discomforting as it may be, there is a trail leading back to forces within the government. Ben Fenton of *The London Telegraph* reports:

The FBI is concentrating its hunt for the source of the anthrax used to terrorise (sic) America on laboratories used by the CIA and British government scientists.

Only five laboratories, including the defence science and technology laboratories at Porton Down, Salisbury, have been found to have spores of anthrax identical to the bacteria sent through the post to two Democratic senators and news organisations (sic) in New York and Florida (2001, pg 1).

Not only are government-connected laboratories such as those at Porton Down under scrutiny, but the CIA is a focus of the FBI's investigation as well:

> Another focus of the FBI inquiry is the CIA, which has been conducting experiments on anthrax in the interests of defence from germ warfare (2001, pg. 1).

Where exactly did the CIA and Porton Down receive their anthrax samples? Fenton provides an answer:

> Both Porton Down, directly, and the CIA, indirectly, received their samples of the particular anthrax spores used in the attacks from the US army medical research institute of infectious diseases at Fort Detrick, about 50 miles north of Washington (2001, pg. 1).

It is possible that the anthrax samples could have been stolen. However, the probability of such a scenario is in question. The FBI's attempts to acquire information concerning the security at Porton Down have faced considerable difficulty (Fenton, 2001, pg. 2). It should also be noted that many of the recipients of the anthrax letters were opponents of the government's anti-terrorist measures. One example would be Patrick Leahy, who has objected to a number of the administration's anti-terrorist initiatives. Was the anthrax letter he received a warning to get back in line and obey marching orders?

All of the above points to a very frightening conclusion: there are some factions of government that consider terrorism to be a tool of social engineering. The direction society is being steered by this "tool" is even more frightening. Terrorism is being used to keep the rabble in line on behalf of an elite that wishes to maintain and expand their power. In *The Power Elite*, sociologist C. Wright Mills introduces these powerful individuals:

The power elite is composed of men whose positions enable them to transcend the ordinary environments of ordinary men and women; they are in positions to make decisions having major consequences. Whether they do or do not make such decisions is less important than the fact that they do occupy such pivotal positions: their failure to act, their failure to make decisions, is itself an act that is often of greater consequence than the decisions they do make. For they are in command of the major hierarchies and organizations of modern society. They rule the big corporations. They run the machinery of the state and claim its prerogatives. They direct the military establishment. They occupy the strategic command posts of the social structure, in which are now centered the effective means of the power and the wealth and the celebrity which they enjoy (pg. 3-4).

Paul David Collins

Talk of oligarchs might tend to conjure pictures of medieval feudal lords. However, a Federal Reserve study points out to elitism being alive, well, and existing in the "Land of the Free", the United States. It states:

> ...54 percent of the total net financial assets were held by the 2 percent of families with the greatest amount of such assets and 86 percent by the top 10 percent; 55 percent of the families in the sample had zero or negative net worth.
>
> Viewed from another perspective, these data imply that fewer than 10 percent of families provided more than 85 percent of the net lending by consumers, and more than half of all families were net borrower (Greider, 1987, pg. 39).

In his *Secrets of the Temple*, former *Washington Post* editor William Greider elaborates on the Federal Reserve study:

The ladder of wealth looked like this: at the top were the 10 percent of American families that owned 86 percent of the net financial worth. Next came 35 percent of American families that, on balance, had accumulated nothing.

The 10 percent and, to a lesser degree, the larger group below them were, of course, the main customers for Wall Street investments. Their net financial worth amounted to about $1.6 trillion.

Families in the top 2 percent owned 30 percent of all liquid assets, everything from checking and savings accounts to money-market funds and bank CDs. They also owned 50 percent of the corporate stocks held by individuals, 39 percent of corporate and government bonds, 71 percent of tax-exempt municipals and 20 percent of all the real estate.

The top 10 percent owned 51 percent of short-term financial paper, 72 percent of corporate stocks, 70

percent of bonds, 86 percent of tax-exempt municipals
and 50 percent of all the real property (pg. 39).

This concentration of wealth in so few hands certainly suggests
that there is a ruling class. It is highly naive to believe that this elite
does not wield a great deal of influence over civilization. In her book,
Beyond The Ruling Class: Strategic Elites In Modern Society,
Professor Suzanne Keller states:

The notion of a stratum elevated above the mass of
men may prompt approval, indifference, or despair, but
regardless of how men feel about it, the fact remains
that their lives, fortunes, and fate are and have long
been dependent on what a small number of men in
high places think and do (1963, pg. 3).

It must also be understood that, while some elites can be
categorized as benign, the majority of the hidden oligarchs are
anything but benevolent. In *The Revolt of the Elites and the Betrayal*

of Democracy, Christopher Lasch determined that the elites posed a definite threat:

> Once it was the "revolt of the masses" that was held to threaten social order and the civilizing traditions of Western culture. In our time, however, the chief threat seems to come from those at the top of the social hierarchy, not the masses (1995, pg. 25).

In his book, *Secret and Suppressed: Banned Ideas and Hidden History*, deceased researcher Jim Keith reprinted a document that supposedly records much of the criminal activities of the elite throughout history. Of the manuscript, which he referred to as simply "The Franciscan Document", Keith stated the following:

> It purports to be a secret history of Western civilization gleaned from secret documents in the Vatican library by a member of the Franciscan order. The inked imprint of a Vatican library entrance chit

affixed to the original document and duplicated at the end of the article is a strong indication that the author does have access to Vatican sources...(Keith, 1993, pg. 215).

While some of the document's findings maybe inaccurate or disinformation, its author does provide a very precise description of the psychology of the ruling class. He writes:

> The elite are an insular, clannish clique, given to raging idiosyncrasies and immense deposits of superstition. Their insulation from the rest of us, and from the world which we inhabit, has rendered them emotionally undeveloped, incapable of loving, of caring, of giving—to them, the sacrifice of an innocent is no more noteworthy than swatting of an annoying fly, and eminently more useful (Keith, *Secret and Suppressed,* 1993, pg.234).

The Franciscan's words should not be dismissed as hyperbole. The evidence overwhelmingly supports the contention that those at the top of the global food chain exercise their power to achieve ends that would make the majority of humanity cringe. Professor Suzanne Keller seemed to be recognizing this fact when she wrote the following:

> The exercise of leadership often brings out the worst in men. Ideals and noble aims are forgotten as leaders, driven by vanity and egoism, become entrapped by the temptations of power (1963, pg. 274).

While Mill provides an accurate description, it is written from the standpoint of an outsider. However, some that have been close to the elite have written of their existence, power, and influence as well. Philip Agee was with the CIA for 12 years before he left the Company in disgust. In *Inside the Company: CIA Diary*, Agee addresses the problem of widespread corruption within American governmental organizations: "Reforms of the FBI and the CIA, even the removal of the President from office, cannot remove the problem" (pg. 597). He then states that, to solve the problem, the CIA, FBI, and other security agencies must be "understood as logical, necessary manifestations of a ruling class's determination to retain power and privilege" (pg. 597).

Now, a word of caution must be raised. Agee's contention that all American intelligence agencies have always been machinations of the elite is not entirely correct. Some of the United States' intelligence apparatus was erected because of legitimate national security concerns. Moreover, Agee's demands for socialist revolution reveals his Marxist proclivities (Agee, 1975, pg. 597). Nevertheless, Agee's remarks do confirm the existence of an elite. Even more frightening, his remarks confirm that the elite is willing to use intelligence agencies, which were initially designed to protect the people, to achieve their own goals.

Former Director of the Central Intelligence Agency William Colby also recognized the existence of a network of bluebloods.

When former Nebraska senator and Vietnam War hero John W. DeCamp was looking into elites' involvement in child abuse, drug running, gunrunning, and satanic ritual—murder, Colby warned him of the hidden aristocracy and their power:

"What you have to understand, John, is that sometimes there are forces and events too big, too powerful, with so much at stake for other people or institutions, that you cannot do anything about them, no matter how evil or wrong they are and no matter how dedicated or sincere you are or how much evidence you have. That is simply one of the hard facts of life you have to face. You have done your part. You have tried to expose the evil and wrongdoing. It has hurt you terribly. But it has not killed you up to this point. I am telling you, get out of this before it does. Sometimes things are just too big for us to deal with, and we have to step aside and let history take its course" (DeCamp, 1996, pg. ix—x).

Probably the greatest source of "insider" information comes from Oxford professor and mentor to former President Bill Clinton, the late Carroll Quigley. After being close to the pro-British, anglophile faction of the elite, Quigley wrote:

> There does exist, and has existed for a generation an international Anglophile network which operates, to some extent, in the way the radical Right believes the Communists act. In fact, this network, which we may identify as the Round Table Groups, has no aversion to cooperating with the Communists, or any other groups, and frequently does so. I know of the operations of this network because I have studied it for twenty years and was permitted for two years, in the early 1960's, to examine its papers and secret records. I have no aversion to it and to many of its aims and have, for much of my life, been close to it and to many of its instruments. I have objected, both in the past and

recently, to a few of its policies (notably to its belief that England was an Atlantic rather than a European Power and must be allied, or even federated, with the United States and must remain isolated from Europe), but in general my chief difference of opinion is that it wishes to remain unknown, and I believe its role in history is significant enough to be known (*Tragedy and Hope*, 1966, pg. 950).

Quigley also informs us that the ruling class has a very low opinion of the common people. He voices this elitist sentiment when he refers to the commoners as:

...the petty bourgeoisie, including millions of persons who regard themselves as middle class and are under all the middle-class anxieties and pressures, but often earn less money than unionized laborers. As a result of these things, they are often insecure, envious, filled with hatreds, and are generally the chief recruits for any Radical Right, Fascist, or hate campaigns against any group that is different or which refuses to conform to middle-class values. Made up of clerks, shopkeepers, and vast numbers of office workers in business, government, finance, and education, these tend to regard their white-collar status as the chief value in life, and live in an atmosphere of envy, pettiness, insecurity, and frustration. They form the major portion of the Republican Party's supporters in the towns of America, as they did for the Nazis in Germany thirty years ago (*Tragedy and Hope*, 1966, pg. 1243-1244).

American resistance against attempts to establish world oligarchy is portrayed as:

...a revolt of the ignorant against the informed or educated, of the nineteenth century against the insoluble problems of the twentieth, of the Midwest of

Tom Sawyer against the cosmopolitan East of J.P. Morgan and Company, of old Siwash against Harvard, of the Chicago Tribune against the Washington Post or The New York Times, of simple absolutes against complex relativisms, of immediate final solutions against long-range partial alleviations, of frontier activism against European thought, a rejection, out of hand, of all the complexities of life which had arisen since 1915 in favor of a nostalgic return to the simplicities of 1905, and above all a desire to get back to the inexpensive, thoughtless, and irresponsible international security Of 1880 (Quigley, *Tragedy and Hope*,1966, pg. 979-980).

It is obvious from Quigley's words that the elites believe themselves to be the only ones possessing mature minds. In his classic, *The Best and the Brightest*, Pulitzer Prize winning author David Halberstam examined the American elite, which are collectively known as the Establishment and are fellow travelers of the elites spoken of by Quigley. He noted the elites' arrogance, stating: "It was the Establishment's conviction that it knew what was right and what was wrong for the country" (1972, pg.76). Halberstam went on to assert that the Establishment elitists "are linked to one another rather than to the country; in their minds they become responsible for the country but not responsive to it" (1972, pg. 76).

Such a superiority complex leads even the staunchest supporter to have his doubts. Later in his life, Quigley began to display a change of heart. This came out in his *The Anglo-American Establishment*, where he writes:

No country that values its safety should allow what the Milner Group [the Anglophile elites-ADDED] accomplished in Britain-that is, that a small number of men should be able to wield such power in administration and politics, should be given almost complete control over the publication of the documents relating to their actions, should be able to exercise such influence over the avenues of information that create

public opinion, and should be able to monopolize so

completely the writing and the teaching of the history

of their own period (pg. 197).

The majority of people do not recognize the existence of the elite,

and the elite are not eager to make their presence known. Professor

Keller points out: "Like a secret society, those at the top rarely reveal

the inner workings of their worlds" (1963, pg. 3). Why is the great

mass of human civilization unaware of the oligarchs' presence among

them? In *The Architecture of Modern Political Power*, Daniel

Pouzzner explains why:

The establishment cloaks itself in cultural

camouflage, employing tactics for which it almost

seamlessly maintains plausible deniability. Subtle,

ubiquitous, often implicit propaganda fosters a broad

public acceptance and embrace of the authority of the

establishment, and of the establishment's definitions of

good and evil, preventing the public from seriously contemplating the reality that the establishment is itself quite often evil by its own definition. The establishment reiterates the mantra that the President of the United States is "the leader of the free world", but a free world has no leader. The President of the United States is simply the most obvious spearhead of the authority of the establishment. He gathers strength at the expense of the world's freedom.

Generally, an errant public attributes the results of the establishment's meddlesome actions to happenstance, or to motives viewed as essentially innocuous or virtuous. The design is irrefutably evident only in the pattern of results, or by actually showing proof of meddling. The public has been systemically conditioned to ignore such patterns, and to condemn those who draw attention to them (derisively calling them "conspiracy theorists"). Thus, controlling access to and dissemination of information that constitutes proof of meddling suffices in large part to protect the establishment program from exposure. The compartmentalization of the establishment's covert apparatus assures that those exposures which do transpire cause only limited damage (pg. 16).

So effective has been the elites' methods of concealing themselves that many of their lackeys are not even aware of the fact that they are mere marionettes. C. Wright Mills explains:

> The truth about the nature and the power of the elite is not some secret which men of affairs know but will not tell. Such men hold quite various theories about their own roles in the sequence of event and decision. Often they are uncertain about their roles, and even more often they allow their fears and their hopes to affect their assessment of their own power. No matter how great their actual power, they tend to be less acutely aware of it than of the resistances of others

to its use. Moreover, most American men of affairs have learned well the rhetoric of public relations, in some cases even to the point of using it when they are alone, and thus coming to believe it. The personal awareness of the actors is only one of the several sources one must examine in order to understand the higher circles. Yet many who believe that there is no elite, or at any rate none of any consequence, rest their argument upon what men of affairs believe about themselves, or at least assert in public (pg. 4).

The elites' successful obfuscation of their presence has prevented the majority from realizing that the activities these would-be rulers engage in are tantamount to a war on the rest of humanity. The war constitutes a conspiracy, but not one in the conventional sense. When one hears the word conspiracy, pictures of popular television shows such as *X-Files, Dark Skies,* and *Millennium* are usually the first things that come to mind. H.G. Wells was a member of two elitist groups, the Fabian Society and the Coefficient Clubs. He was also the mentor of two children from an oligarchical dynasty, Aldous and Julian Huxley. In *Anticipations of the Reaction of Mechanical and Scientific Progress Upon Human Life and Thoughts*, Wells painted quite a different picture. Referring to the blueblood plot as an "Open Conspiracy", Wells wrote:

> The Open Conspiracy will appear first, I believe as a conscious organization of intelligent, and in some cases, wealthy men, as a movement having distinct social and political aims, confessedly ignoring most of the existing apparatus of political control, or using it only as an incidental implement in the stages, a mere movement of a number of people in a certain direction, who will presently discover, with a sort of a surprise the common object toward which they are all moving. In all sorts of ways, they will be influencing and controlling the ostensible government (1902, pg. 285).

In *The Architecture of Modern Political Power*, MIT graduate and systems expert Daniel Pouzzner reiterates Wells' contention:

> The establishment program is not quite a traditional conspiracy. As in many, its members do not all know each other, have sometimes conflicting conceptions of what is to be done, and have sometimes conflicting agendas. From here, the distinctions mount. It is a largely "open" conspiracy, in that much of its membership, structure, methods, and operations, are matters of public record, however scattered and obscure (pg. 31).

Later in his voluminous tract, Pouzzner reinforces the previous statement:

> Obviously, I do not propose that a monolithic, unerring conspiracy is at work, nor do I propose that all of the events which favor the establishment were

instigated by the establishment. Instead, what this document reveals is a network of affiliations and alliances, some strong and some weak, some advertised and some secret, that is working toward a common goal of world rule by oligarchy, with varying degrees of coordination, coherency, and internal contention. It is a conspiracy, but a largely open one, and one of humans, hence neither monolithic nor unerring. Moreover, the core of the establishment has nothing approaching absolute authority. Even the most powerful among them-the first-tier international bankers and the intelligence apparatus they largely control-must often "sugar-coat" their directives, and must always choose them carefully (pg. 14).

Radio talk show host Rush Limbaugh has long held that the idea there is a conspiracy is nothing more than the product of paranoid imaginations. Yet, on his February 7, 1997 program, the neo-conservative made an observation that buttresses conspiracy researcher Pouzzner's above contention. The situation he describes also bears eerie resemblance to the organizational dynamic intrinsic to Well's "open conspiracy":

> You see, if you amount to anything in Washington these days, it is because you have been plucked or handpicked from an Ivy League school-Harvard, Yale, Kennedy School of Government-you've shown an aptitude to be a good Ivy League type, and so you're plucked so-to-speak, and you are assigned success. You are assigned a certain role in government somewhere, and then your success is monitored and tracked, and you go where the pluckers and the handpickers can put you (Cuddy, 1999, pg. 167).

According to H.G. Wells, the "Open Conspiracy's":

> ...main political idea, its political strategy, is to weaken, efface, incorporate, or supersede existing

governments (The Open Conspiracy, 2002 edition, pg. 121).

This objective can be partially accomplished through the creation and use of terrorist networks, both "left-wing" and "right-wing", to compel the "rabble" to willfully trade freedoms for security. Through this method, the target government is transformed into a mere prostitute of the few. The elites have traditionally controlled and funded movements involved in terrorism. The anti-government counter-culture movement of the 1960's is no exception to this rule. In the radical treatise *Do It!*, revolutionary leader of the Yippies Jerry Rubin writes:

> The hip capitalists have some allies within the revolutionary community: longhairs who work as intermediaries between the kids on the street and the millionaire businessmen.

Rubin also states: "The John Birch Society understands the world we live in better than fools like Arthur Schlesinger Jr. and Max Lerner who don't know what…is happening" (pg. 148). Gary Allen's *None Dare Call It Conspiracy* best sums up the John Birch Society's position on the sixties counterculture:

What we are witnessing is the Communist tactic of pressure from above and pressure from below, described by Communist historian Jan Kozak as the device used by the Reds to capture control of Czecho-Slovakia. The pressure from above comes from secret, ostensibly respectable Comrades in the government and Establishment, forming, with radicalized mobs in the streets below, a giant pincer around middle-class society. The street rioter are pawns, shills, puppets, and dupes for an oligarchy of elitist conspirators working above to turn America's limited government into an unlimited government with total control over our lives and property.

The American middle-class is being squeezed to death by a vise...In the streets we have avowed revolutionary groups such as the Students for a Democratic Society (which was started by the League for Industrial Democracy, a group with strong C.F.R. [The Council on Foreign Relations, an organization which acts as a conduit for several elitist interests-ADDED] ties), the Black Panthers, the Yippies, the Young Socialist Alliance. These groups chant that if we don't "change" America, we will lose it. "Change" is a word we hear over and over. By "change" these groups mean Socialism. Virtually all members of these groups sincerely believe that they are fighting the Establishment. In reality they are an indispensable ally of the Establishment in fastening Socialism on all of us. The naïve radicals think that under Socialism the "people" will run everything. Actually, it will be a clique of Insiders in total control, consolidating and controlling all wealth. That is why these schoolboy

141

Lenins and teenage Trotskys are allowed to roam free and are practically never arrested or prosecuted. They are protected. If the Establishment wanted the revolutionaries stopped, how long do you think they would be tolerated?

Instead, we find that most of these radicals are the recipients of largesse from major foundations or are receiving money from the government through the War on Poverty. The Rothschild-Rockefeller-C.F.R. Insiders at the top "surrender to the demands" for Socialism from the mobs below. The radicals are doing the work of those whom they hate the most.

Remember Bakunin's charge that Marx's followers had one foot in the bank and the other in the Socialist movement (pg. 124-125).

Are these the rants of paranoid right-wingers, or is there evidence to support Allen's contentions? Of course, such an assertion is unthinkable to those on the left wing. How could socialism be an instrument designed by the oligarchs to enslave the masses? Socialism is the cause of benevolent Robin Hoods, isn't it? This has been the traditional contention of the left. However, Librarian of Congress James Billington (who certainly cannot be called a conspiracy theorist) describes the prototypical nineteenth-century European revolutionary. This bringer of socialism was:

> ...a thinker lifted up by ideas, not a worker or peasant bent by toil. He was part of a small elite whose story must be told "from above", much as it may displease those who believe that history in general (and revolutionary history in particular) is basically made by socio-economic pressures "from below" (1980, pg. 3).

Billington contends that the major icons of the revolution, such as Marx and Lenin, "were largely middle-class, male intellectuals..." (1980, pg. 5). So much for an uprising of the common man to upset the power of his capitalist masters. Forces "from above" would continue to control and manipulate the extreme left well into the twentieth century. As was previously stated, the activists of the sixties counterculture movement fell into this puppet category. What follows are some significant examples that substantiate this claim.

In his *The Strawberry Statement: Notes of A College Revolutionary*, former revolutionary Kunen gives us the following account of the 1968 S.D.S. (Students for a Democratic Society) national convention:

> Also at the convention, men from Business International Roundtables-the meetings sponsored by the Business International for their client groups and heads of government-tried to buy up a few radicals. These men are the world's leading industrialists and they convene to decide how our lives are going to go. These are the boys who wrote the Alliance for Progress. They're the left wing of the ruling class.

They agreed with us on black control and student control...

They want McCarthy in. They see fascism as the threat, see it coming from Wallace. The only way McCarthy could win is if the crazies and young radicals act up and make Gene more reasonable. They offered to finance our demonstrations in Chicago.

We were also offered Esso (Rockefeller) money. They want us to make a lot of radical commotion so they can look more in the center as they move to the left (pg. 116).

Another individual to discover this connection between the elite and the revolutionary community was undercover police intelligence operative David Gumaer. Gumaer took part in SDS demonstrations. Gumaer states that he:

...wondered where the money was coming from for all this activity, and soon discovered it came through radicals via the United Nations, from the Rockefeller Foundation, the Ford Foundation, United Auto Workers, as well as cigar boxes of American money from the Cuban embassy (Epperson, 1985, pg. 403).

The evidence indicated that violence on the part of the counter-culture was fueled by money from the ruling class. In 1970, Ohio legislators received a shock from a briefing, which included an Illinois commission report that addressed SDS uprisings on Ohio campuses. The report revealed: "...that $192,000 in Federal money and $85,000 in Carnegie Foundation funds were paid to [the] Students for a Democratic Society...during the fall of 1969" (Epperson, 1985, pg. 403).

All of the left's acts of domestic terrorism only helped to consolidate power for the elite. In front of the House and Senate Internal Security Committees, former Communist Party member and FBI informant James Kirk testified:

Young people have no conception of the conspiracy's strategy of pressure from above, pressure from below, as well outlined in Jan Kozak's book, And Not a Shot Was Fired. They have no idea they are playing into the hands of the Establishment they claim to hate.

The radicals think they are fighting the forces of the super-rich, like Rockefeller and Ford, and don't realize that it is precisely such forces which are behind their own revolution, financing it, and using it for their own purposes (Griffin, 1995, pg. 107-108).

Of course, there were some occasions where revolutionaries began to catch on. One revolutionary who began to become wise to the Establishment's manipulation of the movement was Stokely Carmichael, leader of the SNCC. James Kirk relates his story:

Mr. Carmichael was obviously in the middle of something very important which made him more nervous and tense than in the past...He started speaking of things which he said he could not have said before because his research was not finished...

He repeated the line from the song he liked so well, "Something is happening here, but you don't know what it is, do you, Mr. Jones?" He kept hitting on the theme that a very large monopoly capitalist money group, the bankers to be exact, was instrumental in fomenting (the) idea that the Jews are the ones actually behind the oppression of the blacks...In the agencies of this power, he cited banks, the chief among which were Morgan Guaranty Trust and Chase Manhattan. And the foundations connected with these monoliths (Griffin, 1995, pg. 108).

What became of Mr. Carmichael after he came forth with this startling revelation? Author Des Griffin informs us: "Within weeks

Carmichael had been mysteriously removed from SNCC and the Black Panthers. He had learned too much" (pg. 108)!

It seems that Oswald Spengler was on to something when he wrote:

> There is no proletarian, not even a communist, movement that has not operated in the interest of money, in the directions indicated by money, and for the time permitted by money—and that, without the idealist amongst its leaders having the slightest suspicion of the fact (pg. 402).

Through the counterculture left, the oligarchs were able to neutralize grass root attempts to resist plutocracy. The ruling classers used the movement to induce a paradigm shift. Confidence in America's Constitutional Republican form of government was considerably eroded. In addition, more power was concentrated into the hands of government, an entity the elitists could control. Both outcomes worked in accordance with the elite's criteria for maintaining and strengthening their power. Today, many of the baby-boomers have burnt out, went home, and are sleeping off their bad trips. Some have even attempted to climb the Establishment ladder (the Clintons, for instance, traded in their beads and saddles so they could put condoms on the White House Christmas tree). The majority of them have never realized how they were used. Today, when one studies right wing terrorism, it becomes apparent that the story is not much different.

When looking at the oligarchs' involvement in the creation of right-wing terrorism, one must revisit the Oklahoma City bombing. Recall Reverend Millar's bizarre religion known as Christian Identity. This belief system is a theological tributary of British-Israelism, which was a creation of the British faction of the elite. Researcher Anton Chaitkin elaborates:

> It is necessary first to bring to light a myth known
>
> as British Israelism, which stands behind

Pentecostalism. This is an evil piece of historical race gossip, spread into American religion, into the ranks of American populists, poisoning the minds of separatists and Armageddon terrorists.

The British monarchy and its prime ministers and Foreign Office fabricated British Israelism in the nineteenth century, from earlier versions of the story. They claimed that Queen Victoria was descended from the Biblical King David, and was thus a descendant of the Davidic family tree that produced Jesus. They taught that the tribes of Israel wandered into northern Europe; that by this supposed genealogy, the British are the real Chosen People, and the British Empire is thus God's empire.

The modern Jews, by this British account, are not the historical Hebrews of Old Testament Israel, but rather, the British are. But, says the British Israel myth, in a leap of logic, the Jews need to be put into

Palestine, to fulfill prophecy, get slaughtered in a war with the Muslims, and bring about the End Times.

To provide fuel for this mythology, the royal family asked the British Grand Lodge of Freemasonry to establish the Palestine Exploration Fund. In the 1870s, they dispatched soldier-archeologists to the Holy Land, to dig up supposed religious relics that might impress the cheap fancies of the beggarly masses (pg. 13-14).

This British Israelism would be transmitted to the United States, where it would play a significant role in the formation of Pentecostalism. Chaitkin goes into this relationship:

According to Pentecostal lore, the movement began when a woman spoke in tongues in the church of Charles Fox Parham in Topeka, Kansas, in 1901. Reverend Parham spread the method until it blossomed in the famous Azusa Street, Los Angeles, revival of 1906; from there, disciples took it around the world.

During the year preceeding (sic) the launch-time, Parham had caught fire with British Israelism. He had been indoctrinated into the Empire's mystery cult by emissaries of one Frank Sandford, who ran a cult center called Shiloh, near Durham, Maine. Parham made a pilgrimage and studied under Sandford at Shiloh, after which the two of them went on tour through Canada.

Sandford had made the New England Toryism of his fancy Anglophile family relations into a career, traveling back and forth to England, working to inculcate Americans into the British Empire gospel (pg. 15).

The Pentecostal movement would go on to act as a major disseminator of British Israelism, resulting in a rash of violent white supremacist groups. In an interview on the July 30, 1997 program of

EIR Talks, former political prisoner and dissident Lyndon LaRouche pointed towards this strain of religious irrationalism as a major source of terrorism in the United States:

"The greatest threat from terrorism in the United States comes from people who are associated with a British Church of England-run Pentecostalist movement inside the United States. It is this apparatus which has structured the militias. Now, most people in the militia movement, or associated with it, have no part of the intentions of those who are behind it, particularly that section in the Episcopal Church, or Pat Robertson, who's part of this same movement, who are barking...authentically barking...Penticostalists, who, with their connections with the military, deeply embedded in the military, including the...corps of chaplains in the U.S. military, are largely controlled, presently, by outright barking Pentecostalists...This is the...main source of the internal threat of the potential for terrorism, and other kinds of treason inside the United States, today" (Chaitkin, 1997, pg. 1).

The author did not include the above information to act as a sweeping condemnation of practitioners of the Pentecostal faith. Many Pentecostalists can only be characterized as deeply spiritual and highly moral. Nor are the above statements meant to act as a sweeping condemnation of those individuals involved in citizen militias. Many militias are made up of law-abiding citizens that totally reject racism and terrorism as a legitimate form of activism. The inclusion of the above material is meant to point towards the involvement of power elites in producing the ideology behind right-wing terrorism. The federally protected Elohim City, with its leader, FBI informant Reverend Millar, were all adherents of Christian Identity, an offshoot of the British Israelism. It could very well be that the Oklahoma City bombing was Oligarch-inspired.

Are there any ties between the power elites and the current terrorist network? The answer to that question lies with the Bush dynasty. Neither Bush Sr. nor Bush Jr. can be described as presidents in the Lincoln tradition. They do not come from lower class backgrounds and modest upbringings. Webster Tarpley and Anton Chaitkin's in depth investigation of George Sr. led them to propose the following in their excellent *George Bush: The Unauthorized Biography*: "One of our basic theses is that George Bush is, and considers himself to be, an oligarch" (pg. 9). In an article for the London *Daily Mail*, Peter Allen points out a connection between George W. Bush and Osama's brother, Salem Bin Laden:

Incredibly, Salem went on to become a business partner of the man who is leading the hunt for his brother. In the 1970s, he and George W. Bush were founders of the Arbusto Energy oil company in Mr. Bush's home state of Texas (pg. 1).

Allen goes into detail:

As he built his own business empire, Salem Bin Laden had an intriguing relationship with the president-to-be.

In 1978, he appointed James Bath, a close friend of Mr. Bush who served with him in the Air National Guard, as his representative in Houston, Texas.

It was in that year that Mr. Bath invested $50,000...in Mr. Bush's company, Arbusto. It was never revealed whether he was investing his own money or somebody else's.

There was even speculation that the money might have been from Salem. In the same year, Mr. Bath bought Houston Gulf Airport on behalf of the Saudi Arabian multimillionaire. Three years ago, Mr. Bush said the $50,000 investment in Arbusto was the only financial dealing he had with Mr. Bath (pg. 2).

The connection between the Bin Ladens and the Bush family does not end with Arbusto Energy. On the BBC's Newsnight program, Greg Palast stated:

> Young George also received fees as director of a subsidiary of Carlyle Corporation, a little known private company which has, in just a few years of its founding, become one of America's biggest defence contractors. His father, Bush Senior, is also a paid advisor. And what became embarrassing was the revelation that the Bin Ladens held a stake in Carlyle, sold just after September 11 ("Has someone been sitting on the FBI", 2001, pg. 5).

These business connections may explain why the Bush Administration frustrated the FBI's efforts to investigate Abdullah and Omar Bin Laden. Investigations may have demonstrated that Osama was not the "black sheep" of the family. Instead, they may have shown that terrorism was actually the Bin Laden family business. This would have associated the Bush family with terrorists, something the current President could not allow to happen.

For neo-conservatives, the portrait of the Bush family as a criminal syndicate with ties to questionable characters is reprehensible. However, this contention can be based upon a major precedent. Webster Tarpley and Anton Chaitkin's investigation into former President George Herbert Walker Bush's background led to a startling discovery: "The President's family fortune was largely a result of the Hitler project" (1992, pg. 28). What exactly was the "Hitler project"? The project was the Union Banking Corporation, a front for Fritz Thyssen, the most significant financier of Adolf Hitler's Germany (1992, pg. 28). George Sr.'s father, Prescott Bush, was a director of this corporation (1992, pg. 26). All the stock shares in Union Banking Corporation: "were owned by Prescott Bush, E. Roland 'Bunny' Harriman, three Nazi executives, and two other associates of Bush" (1992, pg. 28).

The Union Banking Corporation played a vital role in the rise of Nazism in Germany. An investigation by the U.S government in 1942 found: "that Bush's Nazi-front bank was an interlocking concern with the *Vereinigte Stahlewerke* (United Steel Works Corporation or **German Steel Trust**) led by Fritz Thyssen and his two brothers"(1992, pg. 29). A post-war government investigation found that *Vereinigte Stahlewerke* had produced:

50.8% of Nazi Germany's pig iron

41.4% of Nazi Germany's universal plate

36.0% of Nazi Germany's heavy plate

38.5% of Nazi Germany's galvanized sheet

45.5% of Nazi Germany's pipes and tubes

22.1% of Nazi Germany's wire

35.0 % of Nazi Germany's explosives (1992, pg. 29).

These activities were considered so criminal that, on October 20, 1942, the U.S. government seized the Union Banking Corporation under the *Trading with the Enemy Act* (1992, pg. 26). The Bush dynasty's connections with the Bin Ladens suggest that the family's collusion with enemies of the United States has never ceased.

Now, one must re-examine Martin-Baro's previous contention: Terrorism is part and parcel of a "government-imposed sociopolitical project." Returning to this assertion, one is faced with some very disturbing questions. What will be the results of this "government-imposed sociopolitical project"? Where exactly is all of this state-sponsored terrorism leading? Quigley provides a fragmentary glimpse of the outcome in *Tragedy and Hope*. The Oxford professor reveals that a cognitive elite, arbitrarily dubbed experts, "...will replace the democratic voter in control of the political system" (*Tragedy and Hope*, 1966, pg. 866). H.G. Wells spoke of this democracy of "experts":

> The world's political organization will be democratic, that is to say, the government and direction of affairs will be in immediate touch with and responsive to the general thought of the educated whole population (*The Open Conspiracy*, 2002, pg. 26).

Commenting on the above statement by Wells, W. Warren Wagar wrote:

> Read carefully. He did not say the world government would be elected by the people, or that it would even be responsive to the people—just to those who were "educated" (*The Open Conspiracy*, 2002, pg. 26).

With representation for the masses removed from the picture, what kind of life can the common man expect to live? Quigley declares that this will be a system where the individual's:

> ...freedom and choice will be controlled within very narrow alternatives by the fact that he will be numbered from birth and followed, as a number, through his educational training, his required military or other public service, his tax contributions, his health

and medical requirements, and his final retirement and

death benefits (*Tragedy and Hope*, 1966, pg. 866).

There you have it. George Orwell's *1984* built al-Qaida style!

Paul David Collins

Sources Cited

Adler, Freda, Gerhard Mueller, William Laufer, *Criminology*, McGraw Hill, New York, 2001.

Agee, Philip, *Inside the Company: CIA Diary*, Stonehill Publishing Company, New York, 1975.

Allen, Gary, *None Dare Call It Conspiracy*, Concord Press, Rossmoor, California, 1972.

Allen, Peter, "Bin Laden's family link to Bush", http://www.infowars.com/saved%20pages/Prior_Knowledge/f a..., 2001.

Arney, George, "US planned attack on Taleban", http://news.bbc.co.uk/hi/english/south_asia/newsid_1550000/1 550366.stm, September 18, 2001.

Associated Press, "Bush was warned of a plot before Sept. 11", Springfield News-Sun, May 16, 2002: pg. 1.

Bamford, James, *Body of Secrets: Anatomy of the Ultra-Secret National Security Agency*, Doubleday, 2001.

Billington, James, *Fire in the Minds of Men: Origins of the Revolutionary Faith*, Basic Books Inc., New York, 1980.

165

Blum, Bill (translator), "Interview of Zbigniew Brzezinski",

http://groups.yahoo.com/group/konformist/message/2429,

January 15-21, 1998.

Bone, James, "US 'let Taleban men escape'",

http://www.thetimes.co.uk/article/0,,3-2002033128,00.html,

January 21, 2002.

Brzezinski, Zbigniew, *The Grand Chessboard: American Primacy
and Geostrategic Objectives*, Basic Books, 1997.

Chaitkin, Anton, "British Subversion of the United States: Who is
wagging your neighbor's tongue? The militias and
Pentecostalism", http://www.larouchepub.com/ahc.html,
September 10, 1997.

Chomsky, Noam, *Deterring Democracy*, Hill and Wang, New York,
1992.

CNN, "Transition of Power: President—Elect Bush Meets With
Congressional Leaders on Capitol Hill",
http://www.cnn.com/TRANSCRIPTS/0012/18/nd.01.html,
December 18, 2000.

Cuddy, Dennis, *Secret Records Revealed: The Men, The Money, and The Methods Behind the New World Order,* Hearthstone Publishing, Oklahoma, 1999.

DeCamp, John W., *The Franklin Cover—Up: Child Abuse, Satanism, and Murder in Nebraska*, AWT Inc., Nebraska, 1996.

Drexler, Madeline, *Secret Agents: The Menace of Emerging Infections*, Joseph Henry Press, Washington D.C., 2002.

Epperson, Ralph, *The Unseen Hand*, Publius Press, Tucson, Arizona, 1985.

Evans-Pritchard, Ambrose, *The Secret Life of Bill Clinton: The Unreported Stories*, Regnery Publishing, Washington, 1997.

Fainaru, Steve and James V. Grimaldi, "FBI knew Terrorists Were Using Flight Schools", http//www.washingtonpost.com/ac2/wp-dyn/A10840-2001Sep22?language=printer, September 23, 2001.

Fenton, Ben, "CIA links Porton Down to anthrax attacks", http://www.portal.telegraph.co.uk/news/main.html?xml=/news/2001/12/17/wthrax17.xml&sSheet=/portal/2001/12/17/por_right..., 2001.

Greider, William, *Secrets of the Temple: How the Federal Reserves Runs the Country*, Simon and Schuster, New York, 1987.

Griffin, Des, *Fourth Reich of the Rich*, Emissary Publications, Oregon, 1995.

Grigg, William Norman, "Battle Lines in the Drug War", New American, October 27, 1997: pg. 11-16.

Halberstam, David, *The Best and the Brightest*, Fawcett Crest, Connecticut, 1972.

Jones, Alex, "Alex Jones Interviews David Shippers: Government Knowledge of Pending Terrorist Attacks", http://www.infowars.com/transcript_schippers.html, October 10, 2001.

Joshi, Manoj, "India helped FBI trace ISI-terrorist links", http://www.timesofindia.com/articleshow.asp?catkey=-2128936835&art_id=1454238160&..., October 9, 2001.

Juergensmeyer, Mark, "Understanding the New Terrorism", *Current History*, April 2000.

Ijaz, Mansoor, "Clinton Let Bin Laden Slip Away and Metastasize",
http://www.latimes.com/templates/misc/printstory.jsp?=1a%2
D000096561dec05, December 5, 2001.

Keith, Jim, *Secret and Suppressed: Banned Ideas and Hidden
History*, Feral House, Portland, Oregon, 1993.

Keith, Jim, *OKBomb!*, Illuminet Press, Lilburn, Georgia, 1996.

Keith Jim, *Casebook on Alternative Three*, Illuminet Press, Lilburn,
Georgia, 1994.

Keller, Suzanne, *Beyond The Ruling Class: Strategic Elites In
Modern Society*, Random House, New York, 1963.

Kick, Russ, "September 11, 2001: No Surprise",
http://www.loompanics.com/Articles/September11.html,
2002.

Kozak, Jan, *And Not a Shot is Fired*, Connecticut, The Long House,
Inc., 1957.

Kunen, James, *The Strawberry Statement*, Random House, New York,
1968.

Lasch, Christopher, *The Revolt of the Elites and the Betrayal of
Democracy*, W.W. Norton and Company, New York, 1995.

Levine, Michael and Laura Kavanau, *The Triangle of Death*,

    Delacorte Press, New York, 1996.

Margolis, Eric, "America's New War: A Progress Report",

    http://www.commondreams.org/views01/1209-02.htm, 2001.

Marrs, Texe, *Circle of Intrigue*, Living Truth Publishers, Austin,

    Texas, 1995.

McGee, Jim, "An Intelligence Giant in the Making",

    http://www.washingtonpost.com/wp-dyn/articles/A33340-

    2001Nov3.html?id=6846, November 4, 2001.

Moran, Michael, "Bin Laden comes home to roost",

    http//www.msnbc.com/news/190144.asp?cp1=1, August 24,

    1998.

Page, Clarence, "Ashcroft shows his ugly side", Springfield News—

    Sun, December 13, 2001: page 10.

Palast, Gregory, "FBI And US Spy Agents Say Bush Spiked Bin

    Laden Probes Before 11 September",

    http://www.gregpalast.com/printerfriendly.cfm?artid=103,

    November 7, 2001.

Palast, Gregory, "Has someone been sitting on the FBI?" http://news.bbc.co.uk/hi/english/events/newsnight/newsid_164 5000/1645527.stm.

Pouzzner, Daniel, *The Architecture of Modern Political Power: The New Feudalism*, http://www.mega.nu:8080, 2001.

Pike, Albert, *Morals and Dogma*, L.H. Jenkins, Inc., Richmond, Virginia, 1942.

Quigley, Carroll, *Tragedy and Hope: A History of the World in Our Time*, MacMillan Company, New York, 1966.

Quigley, Carroll, *The Anglo-American Establishment*, Books in Focus, New York, 1981.

Rivero, Michael, "Fake Terror-Road to Dictatorship" http://www.what reallyhappened.com/ARTICLE5/index.html, 2001.

Robinson, Gwen, "CIA 'ignored warning' on al Qaeda", http://news.ft.com/gx.cgi/ftc?pagename=View&c=Article&cid =FT3KP6GQCWC&live=tr..., January 12, 2002.

Paul David Collins

Rose, Toby, "CIA Agent 'met Bin Laden in July",

http://www.thisislondon.com/dynamic/news/story.html?

in_review_id=470280&in_review...., October 31, 2001.

Rubin, Jerry, *Do It!*, Ballantine Books, New York, 1970.

Shackley, Theodore, *The Third Option: An Expert's Provocative*

Report on an American View of Counterinsurgency

Operations, Dell Publishing, New York, 1981.

Shirer, William, *The Rise and Fall of the Third Reich*, Touchstone,

Simon and Schuster, 1959.

Spengler, Oswald, *The Decline of the West Volume 2: Perspectives of*

World History, Alfred A. Knopf Inc., New York, 1928.

Stephens, Joe and David B. Ottaway, "From the U.S.A., the ABCs of

jihad", http://stacks.msnbc.com/news/728439.asp, 2002.

Unsigned Document, "Serpico slams terror steps", Springfield News-

Sun, July 7, 2002: pg. 2.

The Times of India, "CIA worked in tandem with Pak to create Taliban",

http://www.infowars.com/Saved_Articles/7%20March%2020

01%20%20CIA%20worked...,March 7, 2001.

Wells, H.G., with a critical introduction by W. Warren Wagar, *The Open Conspiracy: H.G. Wells on World Revolution*, Praeger Studies on the 21st Century, Connecticut, 2002 edition.

Wells, H.G., *Anticipations of the Reaction of Mechanical and Scientific Progress Upon Human Life and Thought*, Harper and Row, 1902.

Wheeler, Larry, "Pensacola NAS link faces more scrutiny", http://www.infowars.com/saved%20pages/Prior_Knowledge/pensacola_link.htm, September 17, 2001.

Paul David Collins

About the Author

Paul Collins has studied suppressed history and the shadowy undercurrents of world political dynamics for roughly eleven years. In 1999, he completed his Associates of Arts and Science degree. He will soon complete his Bachelor's degree with a major in Communications and a minor in Political Science. He is a member of the Phi Theta Kappa and Phi Kappa Phi honor societies. Throughout the course of his ongoing college career, he has extensively researched political science, criminal justice, psychology, philosophy, and religion.

Printed in the United States
25875LVS00003B/227

9 781403 367990